A WORLD BANK COUNTRY STUDY

El Salvador
Meeting the Challenge of Globalization

The World Bank
Washington, D.C.

Copyright © 1996
The International Bank for Reconstruction
and Development/ THE WORLD BANK
1818 H Street, N.W.
Washington, D.C. 20433, U.S.A.

World Bank Country Studies are among the many reports originally prepared for internal use as part of the continuing analysis by the Bank of the economic and related conditions of its developing member countries and of its dialogues with the governments. Some of the reports are published in this series with the least possible delay for the use of governments and the academic, business and financial, and development communities. The typescript of this paper therefore has not been prepared in accordance with the procedures appropriate to formal printed texts, and the World Bank accepts no responsibility for errors. Some sources cited in this paper may be informal documents that are not readily available.

The World Bank does not guarantee the accuracy of the data included in this publication and accepts no responsibility whatsoever for any consequence of their use. The boundaries, colors, denominations, and other information shown on any map in this volume do not imply on the part of the World Bank Group any judgment on the legal status of any territory or the endorsement or acceptance of such boundaries.

The material in this publication is copyrighted. Requests for permission to reproduce portions of it should be sent to the Office of the Publisher at the address shown in the copyright notice above. The World Bank encourages dissemination of its work and will normally give permission promptly and, when the reproduction is for noncommercial purposes, without asking a fee. Permission to copy portions for classroom use is granted through the Copyright Clearance Center, Inc., Suite 910, 222 Rosewood Drive, Danvers, Massachusetts 01923, U.S.A.

The complete backlist of publications from the World Bank is shown in the annual *Index of Publications*, which contains an alphabetical title list (with full ordering information) and indexes of subjects, authors, and countries and regions. The latest edition is available free of charge from the Distribution Unit, Office of the Publisher, The World Bank, 1818 H Street, N.W., Washington, D.C. 20433, U.S.A., or from Publications, The World Bank, 66, avenue d'Iéna, 75116 Paris, France.

ISSN: 0253-2123

Library of Congress Cataloging-in-Publication Data

El Salvador : meeting the challenge of globalization.
     p. cm. — (A World Bank country study)
   Includes bibliographical references.
   ISBN 0-8213-3720-3
   1. El Salvador—Economic policy. 2. Structural adjustment
(Economic policy)—El Salvador. 3. Economic stabilization—El
Salvador. I. Grandolini, Gloria M. II. World Bank. III. Series.
HC148.E437 1996
338.97284— dc20
                             96-32304
                              CIP

CONTENTS

TEXT TABLES

TEXT FIGURES

ANNEX TABLES

ANNEX FIGURES

PREFACE

Stabilization and adjustment measures implemented since 1989 and the return to peace have laid the foundations for sustained growth in El Salvador. However, there is a need for more rapid growth to consolidate peace and alleviate poverty. Facing a turning point, El Salvador has decided to take a dramatic leap forward to try to rise above this relative success and rapidly catch up with high-performing economies. The vision is to achieve rapid and equitable growth by increasing global competitiveness and entering a new stage of development. El Salvador is currently undertaking bold economic reforms to become a more open economy with a dynamic export-oriented private sector keyed into international markets and a small and strong State facilitating private sector activities.

The premise of this report is that El Salvador's vision may be attained. The return to peace and changes in the global economic environment provide favorable opportunities. However, for it to become a reality two main challenges must be met. First, peace must be consolidated. Bold economic reforms will be a key factor in accelerating investment, exports, and growth, but not a sufficient one. Persistent security concerns must be eliminated to lower the risks of operating in the country and attract investors. At the root of the civil conflict were both economic and social problems, particularly land-related issues and income inequalities.[1] Only a combination of economic growth and the implementation of policies specifically addressing social and land-related issues will ensure continued social peace. The second challenge is to seize the opportunities arising from globalization by removing existing constraints to increased competitiveness and accelerated growth. Key constraints lie in weak support systems for private enterprise that inhibit accumulation, productivity growth, and international competitiveness. The Government can remove these constraints by acting in two areas: reforming the State and implementing policy reforms supportive of outward-oriented private sector-led growth.

This report seeks to support the Government's reform effort by proposing a policy agenda to increase El Salvador's global competitiveness. It identifies constraints to accelerated outward-oriented private sector-led growth and policy options to address them. Chapter I summarizes developments since 1989 and discusses the genesis, characteristics, and policy implications of the Government's vision and the public-private sector interaction. Chapter II reviews the remaining agenda to further strengthen macroeconomic stability, focusing on the need to improve fiscal performance and to address macroeconomic management concerns associated with high foreign exchange flows. Chapter III discusses policies to develop human resources and increase labor productivity and presents options for infrastructure modernization. Chapter IV discusses policies to improve the legal and regulatory framework. Chapter V reviews options to minimize distortions and remove constraints in the trade regime and to accelerate technological catching up. Chapter VI focuses on measures to strengthen the financial sector to enhance allocation toward high-productivity investments and increase the level of financial savings.

---

[1] Poverty and income inequality issues are covered in "El Salvador - The Challenge of Poverty Alleviation", June 9, 1994, Report No. 12315-ES (The World Bank) and land-related issues are being addressed through on-going (Agricultural Sector Reform Project) and future (Land Administration Project) projects.

ACKNOWLEDGMENTS

This report was prepared by a team led by Gloria M. Grandolini (LA2CO) based on a series of missions to El Salvador during 1993-95 and reflects joint efforts by the Government (GAES/MIPLAN, the Central Bank, and the Ministries of Finance and Economy) and the World Bank. Contributors to the report were: Ian Bannon (Lead Economist, LA2CO); Harold Bedoya (macroeconomic analysis, data, and graphics, LA2CO); Sara Calvo (trade, EDIEM); Richard Clifford (infrastructure, LA2IN); Luis Guasch (labor markets and regulatory framework, LATAD); Andrew Stone (private enterprise survey, PSD); Saud Siddique (capital markets, IFC-CLACM); Charles Thomas (infrastructure, PSD); and the following consultants: Suphan Andic (taxation), Manuel Lasaga (financial sector), and FUSADES (private enterprise survey). The Department Director is Edilberto L. Segura, the Division Chief is Donna Dowsett-Coirolo, and the Lead Economist is Ian Bannon.

CURRENCY EQUIVALENTS AND GLOSSARY

Currency Unit	= colón (c)
US$1.0	= 8.75 (August 1995)
c 1.0	= US$0.11

FISCAL YEAR

January 1 to December 31

GLOSSARY OF ACRONYMS AND ABBREVIATIONS

ANDA	= National Water Company *(Administración Nacional de Acueductos y Alcantarillados)*
ANTEL	= National Telecommunications Administration *(Administración Nacional de Telecomunicaciones)*
BCR	= Central Bank *(Banco Central de Reserva)*
CACM	= Central American Common Market
CEL	= National Power Company *(Comisión Ejecutiva Hidroeléctrica del Río Lempa)*
CENTREX	= Export Processing Center *(Centro de Trámites de Exportaciones)*
CEPA	= National Ports Authority *(Comisión Ejecutiva Portuaria Autónoma)*
FMLN	= Farabundo Marti National Liberation Front *(Frente Farabundo Martí de Liberación Nacional)*
FTZ	= Free Trade Zone
FUSADES	= Salvadoran Foundation for Economic and Social Development
GAES	= Economic and Social Advisory Group *(Grupo Asesor Económico y Social)*
IDB	= Inter-American Development Bank
IMF	= International Monetary Fund
INPEP	= Public Sector Pension Institute *(Instituto de Previsión de Empleados Públicos)*
ISSS	= Social Security Institute *(Instituto de Seguridad Social)*
MIPLAN	= Ministry of Planning
MOE	= Ministry of Education
NAFTA	= North American Free Trade Agreement
NRP	= National Reconstruction Plan
NTBs	= Non-Tariff Barriers
ONI	= National Investment Office *(Oficina Nacional de Inversiones)*
PSMP	= Public Sector Modernization Program
RDC	= Commercial Registry *(Registro de Comercio)*
RER	= Real Exchange Rate
SFF	= Superintendency of the Financial System *(Superintendencia del Sistema Financiero)*
USAID	= United States Agency for International Development
VAT	= Value Added Tax

EXECUTIVE SUMMARY

El Salvador's achievements since 1989 have been formidable but more rapid growth is needed. The Government's vision is to accelerate equitable growth by increasing global competitiveness. The return to peace and changes in the global economic environment provide favorable opportunities. Current bottlenecks are low human and physical resource accumulation, low productivity, and limited outward-orientation. The main challenges are consolidating peace and quickly transforming polices to seize the opportunities arising from globalization. This transformation requires reforming the State and supporting outward-oriented private sector-led growth. To leapfrog into a new stage of development the Government must act quickly and concurrently on six policy areas: enhancing macroeconomic stability; developing human resources and increasing labor productivity; modernizing infrastructure; improving the legal and regulatory framework; facilitating trade and technological innovation; and strengthening the financial sector.

El Salvador's achievements since 1989 have been formidable...

El Salvador has made a dramatic leap forward since the late 1980s. In 1989, the 10 year old civil war was still ongoing, GDP per capita was 15 percent lower than 1978 levels, and a full fledged economic crisis had emerged. By the mid 1990s, the Government had ended the civil war, stabilized the economy and reactivated growth, and initiated a systematic attack on poverty. These efforts have lifted the country from the economic crisis of the 1980s and placed it on a path of relative stability and economic growth.

...but more rapid growth is needed

Notwithstanding these achievements, three considerations have led the Government to reassess the development strategy followed over the last few years. First, even more rapid economic growth is a necessary condition to consolidate peace and alleviate poverty. Although growth improved in the post-war period, GDP per capita remains at pre-war levels and the trickle down effects of prosperity have not yet been felt widely enough. Second, current growth trends may not be sustainable unless exports expand considerably. Third, recent trends in international economic integration - the globalization phenomenon - highlight that to raise welfare developing countries must become globally competitive in technologically more advanced goods and services.

The Government's vision: accelerate equitable growth by increasing global competitiveness

The challenge now facing the Government is to fulfill its vision of raising El Salvador above this relative success by seizing the opportunities arising from globalization and rapidly catching up with high-performing economies. The goal is to achieve rapid and equitable growth by becoming a more open and competitive economy with a dynamic export-oriented private sector keyed into international markets and a small and strong State facilitating private sector activities. This report identifies existing constraints to the achievement of this vision and proposes a policy agenda to increase El Salvador's global competitiveness.

The opportunities: the return to peace and changes in the global economic environment

Domestic and international changes have created opportunities for the attainment of El Salvador's vision:

⇨ in the domestic arena, the return to peace and the implementation of a coherente and comprehensive economic strategy have set the stage for an acceleration of private sector activity and foreign direct investment; and

⇨ in the international arena, globalization - driven by widespread adoption of liberalization policies, buoyant world trade, technological catching up, increasing capital flows, and the internationalizationof services - represents a fundamental opportunity for raising welfare.

⇨ in the domestic arena, the return to peace and the implementation of a coherent and comprehensive economic strategy have set the stage for an acceleration of private sector activity and foreign direct investment; and

⇨ in the international arena, globalization - driven by widespread adoption of liberalization policies, buoyant world trade, technological catching up, increasing capital flows, and the internationalization of services - represents a fundamental opportunity for raising welfare.

The bottlenecks: low accumulation, low productivity, and limited outward-orientation

The experience of high performing economies elsewhere, most notably those in East Asia, suggests that to accelerate growth governments need to focus on augmenting physical and human resource accumulation, enhancing the allocative efficiency and the productivity of resources, and increasing outward orientation.

El Salvador has:

⇨ low investment and savings levels;

⇨ inadequate human capital stock, especially low primary enrollment ratios which do not bode well for a rapid increase in the stock, and low educational quality;

⇨ low allocative efficiency and productivity growth; and

⇨ low exports and limited outward orientation.

Two challenges: consolidating peace ...

Economic reforms will be a key factor in accelerating investment, exports, and growth, but these will not be sufficient. To consolidate peace, lower the risk of doing business in El Salvador, and attract investors, the Peace Accords must also be fully implemented and security concerns addressed. Policies specifically addressing social and land-related issues at the root of the civil war must be implemented.

...and quickly transforming policies to meet the challenge of globalization

El Salvador is currently developing economic reforms to remove existing bottlenecks to increased global competitiveness and accelerated growth. The focus should be on:

⇨ transforming policies and structures to support outward-oriented growth,

⇨ assuring adequate human and physical infrastructure,

⇨ acquiring technology by plugging into the world economy and attracting foreign investment, and

⇨ facilitating resource shifts toward exportable goods and services.

This transformation requires: reforming the State...

To achieve this vision, the interaction and complementarity between the State and the private sector is critical. Key constraints to meeting the challenge of globalization lie in weak support systems for private enterprise that inhibit accumulation, productivity growth, and international competitiveness.

The State should reform itself to ensure the efficient provision of essential public goods and services and to reorient public resources to support economic growth and attend to the most urgent needs of the poor. The public sector should concentrate on core activities, improving the quality, efficiency, and coverage of the services which the State will continue to provide, while working to strengthen its capacity to formulate and implement policies that enable the private sector to thrive. The full and timely implementation of the on-going Public Sector Modernization Program is the necessary condition for successfully entering the new stage of development.

...and supporting outward-oriented private sector-led growth by...

In parallel, the Government should remove existing constraints to the acceleration of outward-oriented private sector-led growth by acting rapidly and concurrently on six fundamental policy areas:
⇨ further enhance the stability of the macroeconomic framework,
⇨ develop human resources and increase labor productivity,
⇨ modernize infrastructure,
⇨ improve the legal and regulatory framework,
⇨ facilitate trade and technological diffusion, and
⇨ strengthen the financial sector.

...Enhancing macroeconomic stability...

In an increasingly more open, integrated, and competitive global economy, economic management must ensure stability to maintain the confidence of domestic and international markets and flexibly respond to capital flows. El Salvador has shown remarkable macroeconomic improvements since 1989 but the Government still needs to:

⇨ strengthen fiscal performance, and
⇨ adjust macroeconomic management to high foreign exchange flows.

Improvements in fiscal performance since 1989 have been impressive, but much remains to be done to address low public savings, low capital expenditures, inertial and inflexible expenditure patterns, and dependence on external financing. A stronger fiscal performance is necessary to: meet peace-related expenditures, address large unmet social needs, and ensure the credibility of exchange rate and monetary policies. Two priority areas should be addressed:
⇨ further increasing tax revenues to augment public savings and decrease reliance on external financing by broadening the tax base, strengthening tax administration, and enforcing compliance; and
⇨ modernizing the public sector to improve efficiency, with particular emphasis on privatization and civil service reform.

Notwithstanding their positive impact on living standards and on the balance of payments, high foreign exchange inflows have complicated macroeconomic management and the attainment of other policy fundamentals. In particular, abundant foreign exchange flows have contributed to inflationary pressures, real exchange rate appreciation and variability, and external sector vulnerability. Sterilization policies - aimed at containing monetary expansion and maintaining a stable nominal exchange rate - have further complicated macroeconomic management by putting pressure on interest rates and on the Central Bank's operational deficit.

Although foreign exchange flows will stabilize at lower growth rates, they are likely to be a permanent feature. This entails a change in the underlying structure of the economy. The challenge is to adjust to the higher level of inflows. While in the short-run, the Government should continue open market operations to sterilize excess inflows, these impose costs in the financial system and have a limited impact. In the long-run, the challenge is to adjust to the higher level of inflows by continuing implementation of policies which, in addition to improving fiscal performance, should aim at:

⇨ raising national savings by: (i) increasing the depth and efficiency of the financial sector; (ii) reforming the social security system; and (iii) increasing public savings;

⇨ containing inflationary pressures by: (i) encouraging higher domestic savings; (ii) lowering government consumption, which is usually biased toward non-traded goods; (iii) fostering private investment, which is usually more traded good-intensive; and (iv) in the longer-term, ensuring that a larger percentage of private inflows are in the form of foreign direct investment; and

⇨ pursuing a credible exchange rate policy while limiting real exchange rate appreciation; the continuation of high inflows and economic growth entail a change in the underlying structure of the economy, and in particular, a lower real exchange rate. To avoid short-run real exchange rate misalignment, the authorities should continue to focus on ensuring consistent macroeconomic polices and moderating inflation. There are a number of policy actions the Government can focus on to generate a long-run real depreciation: (i) accelerate trade liberalization (to increase demand for traded goods); (ii) lower foreign exchange flows by improving fiscal performance and decreasing the external financing needs of the public sector; and (iii) increase national savings; and

⇨ facilitating expansion and diversification of exports, within a framework of a lower real exchange rate by: (i) ensuring a stable macroeconomic environment; (ii) removing general constraints to private investment; and, (iii) removing specific constraints to export growth.

...developing human resources and labor markets...

The labor market appears to be relatively competitive, with wages determined largely by market conditions However, the lack of skilled workers and low labor productivity may be the key bottleneck to accelerating growth. The Government should address these constraints by:

⇨ ensuring a growing supply of skilled labor through education sector reforms;

⇨ enhancing the productivity of existing capital stock by supporting private sector efforts to develop an active and comprehensive training policy; and

⇨ contributing to the quality and efficiency of labor supply through health sector reforms.

In addition, actions should be taken to lower direct and indirect labor costs through wage policy and public sector employment reforms.

...modernizing infrastructure...

El Salvador cannot fulfill its potential for export-led growth without overhauling and modernizing its telecommunications, power, transport, water and waste networks. The poor condition of infrastructure saps the competitiveness of the private sector, as efficient services are increasingly important to firms' capacity to compete in world markets. The foundation for this transformation has been established and some steps have been taken already.

The agenda of comprehensive policy and institutional change in each infrastructure sector involves:

⇨ revising the basic legal framework of governance;

⇨ reforming market structures within sectors;

⇨ articulating in detail the new government role in regulation, particularly to ensure a politically independent approach for formulating tariff policy based on sound economic and financial criteria;

⇨ specifying the financial role of government;

⇨ promoting private sector participation; and

⇨ in those activities which remain, transitionally or for the longer term, under public ownership and operation, restructuring of the responsible entity may be needed to create incentives for efficient, commercial operation and to permit even limited private sector involvement, such as through contracting-out of specific services, or management contracts.

...improving the legal and regulatory framework...

The legal and regulatory framework needs to be revised, focusing on:

⇨ establishing and securing real and intellectual property rights by modernizing the Registry of Real Property and fighting piracy;

⇨ improving contract law by providing general rules for calculating extra-contractual liabilities and damages;

⇨ facilitating company entry, operation, and exit by: (i) further simplifying and speeding up the registration process and centralizing ONI's institutional structure; (ii) strengthening the supervision of companies; (iii) simplifying the Commercial Code by eliminating unnecessary procedures; (iv) harmonizing and simplifying foreign investment rules to eliminate procedural and structural entry barriers; and (v) improving the speed and efficiency of bankruptcy proceedings;

⇨ strengthening competition policy and consumer protection by enacting a modern competition policy and anti-trust legislation addressing monopolistic and restraints of trade practices;

⇨ improving tax rules and administration by: addressing distorted incentives; controlling unfair competition; and diminishing compliance costs; and

⇨ improving the predictability and speed of conflict resolution and of the enforcement of laws and regulations, and fostering the use of arbitration.

...facilitating trade and technological innovation...

A stable macroeconomic environment and the removal of general constraints to private sector development will be key to increase the outward-orientation of the economy. However, to accelerate export supply response, parallel efforts are necessary to address policies and administrative mechanisms which impede the achievement of policy neutrality between domestic and international markets and that negatively influence export competitiveness by raising costs, diminishing quality, and slowing order response time.

The Government can enhance export supply response and competitiveness by:

⇨ deepening and sustaining trade liberalization by moving to a uniform tariff rate, eliminating remaining administrative instruments regulating import flows, and responding to the challenges of NAFTA;

⇨ eliminating remaining policy and institutional obstacles to trade expansion by: (i) further reducing import-related administrative costs and procedures; and (ii) simplifying export-related administrative procedures, addressing issues related to the functioning of the Free Trade Zones and Fiscal Areas, and improving the functioning of the duty drawback system;

⇨ facilitating private sector efforts to gain access to technology and enhancing its capability of adapting to these new technologies by: (i) adopting and maintaining a liberal trade and investment regime; (ii) ensuring supportive human and physical infrastructure; and (iii) supporting private sector initiatives;

⇨ continue strengthening trade negotiation capabilities to take full advantage of opportunities created by the Uruguay Round, the internationalization of services, and regional integration efforts; and

⇨ improving business-government consultation mechanisms.

...and strengthening the financial sector

Financial sector reforms implemented since 1989 have set the foundations for the development of a modern financial system. Nevertheless, more needs to be done to sustain and deepen these reforms and develop a financial system which can support accelerated growth.

Government efforts should continue focusing on:

⇨ improving access to credit by: (i) addressing collateral security issues to ensure effective creation, perfection, and enforcement of security interests; (ii) promoting the use of new financing instruments such as leasing, factoring, and liens on inventory and on commercial equipment; and (iii) promoting access to credit by microenterprises through new approaches, along the lines of successful international experiences;

⇨ further liberalizing and strengthening the banking system to enhance its capacity to absorb large changes in liquidity by: (i) eliminating ownership limitations; (ii) lowering illiquidity risks; (iii) strengthening

supervision; and (iv) establishing a deposit insurance fund; and

⇨ contributing to the development of financial markets by: (i) acting as a catalyst by issuing public securities; (ii) enforcing standards of fairness in trading and broad disclosure of information; (iii) strengthening prudential regulation; and (iv) developing enabling legislation for the reform and more active involvement of institutional investors, such as contractual savings institutions (insurance companies and pension funds) and other financial intermediaries, such as mutual funds and leasing companies.

Seizing opportunities for accelerating growth

Peace and globalization have created new opportunities to accelerate growth but to seize these opportunities the Government must act rapidly and concurrently on all policy areas. El Salvador has an entrepreneurial, innovative, and resilient private sector. If the State is able to consolidate peace, reform itself, and remove constraints to outward-orientation and private sector development, the shared vision for the twenty first century will be within reach.

A Road Map for El Salvador[a]

CONSTRAINTS			RECOMMENDATIONS		
Area	Issues	Priority	Recommendations	Tech. Diffic.	Period of Impl.
MACROECONOMIC FRAMEWORK					
Fiscal Policy	Low public savings; fiscal improvements mostly associated with lower capital expenditures; inertial and inflexible expenditure patterns; and dependence on foreign sources of financing	●●●	Increase tax revenues by broadening the tax base, strengthening tax administration, and enforcing compliance. Modernize the public sector to improve efficiency	●●	MT
Macro Management	High foreign exchange inflows have complicated macroeconomic management and the attainment of a number of policy fundamentals: (i) inflationary pressures; (ii) real exchange rate appreciation and variability; (iii) external viability concerns; and (iv) interest rate pressures.	●●●	In the short-term, continue open market operations to sterilize excess inflows. In the long-run, the challenge is to adjust to the higher level of inflows by continuing the implementation of policies which, in addition to improving fiscal performance, should aim at: (i) encouraging high levels of national savings; (ii) containing inflationary pressures; (iii) pursuing a credible exchange rate policy while limiting real exchange rate appreciation; and (iv) facilitating expansion and diversification of exports, within a framework of a lower real exchange rate.	●●	MT
HUMAN RESOURCES AND LABOR MARKETS					
Human Resources	Low skill level keeps productivity and wages low, limits labor supply for non-traditional export industries; low health levels also lower quality of labor force.	●●●	Re-orient public expenditure to invest more in primary education and health services; allow private provision, explore private and NGO routes to deliver publicly-financed services; and strengthen institutional capacity of Ministries of Education and Health.	●●	LT
	Insufficient levels of on-the job human capital accumulation	●●●	Encourage and support private sector industry-based vocational training	●●	LT

---

[a] The Road Map is an analytical tool to: (i) identify, prioritize, and analyze constraints inhibiting private sector-led growth, (ii) identify solutions and assess their technical feasibility, and (iii) develop a strategic agenda. For each constraint, an assessment is made of the degree of importance and the extent to which relieving the constraint would facilitate private sector growth. Over time, as more important constraints are relieved, less important constraints become more prominent. The categories of importance used are high (●●●), medium (●●), and low (●). High indicates that the constraint is critical and is a binding or very important constraint on firm activity. Medium indicates that the firm can still operate with this constraint, but with a fair amount of difficulty. Low indicates that while the constraint increases firms' difficulties in conducting business, they are able to overcome this constraint with relatively minimal effort. *Technical difficulty* measures the level of specialized expertise required and the administrative difficulty involved in implementation. Finally, for each constraint, the Road Map identifies a period of implementation. This should again reflect two components: sequencing and gestation. The measures of timing are: Short-Term (ST) - less than 1 year; Medium-Term (MT) - 1-3 years; and Long-Term (LT) - more than 3 years. This strategy should give a sense of the time frame in which actions will occur. The final step is to identify who will undertake them.

CONSTRAINTS			RECOMMENDATIONS		
Area	**Issues**	**Priority**	**Recommendations**	**Tech. Diffic.**	**Period of Impl.**
HUMAN RESOURCES AND LABOR MARKETS *(Cont'd)*					
Wage Policies	Sector-specific wage policies, overtime and fringe-benefit provisions cause distortions or artificially increase labor costs.	●●	Unify minimum wage at hourly rate. Permit/encourage productivity-linked compensation. Reduce overtime and night shift wage.	●	ST
Labor Management	Limited use of oral procedures. Lack of compulsory mediation.	●	Expand the use of oral proceedings. Establish a requirement for compulsory arbitration, beyond the essential services clause, with a legal right of appeal. Extend compulsory mediation and arbitration to individual conflict cases.	●●	MT
Public Sector Employment	Public sector employment and wage policies distort labor markets and influence private management practices. Public agencies suffer from personnel management weakness, wage distortions, short working hours, overstaffing, lack of competitive recruitment procedures, lack of incentive-based compensation.	●●●	Strengthen public sector human resource management. Revise Civil Service Law to eliminate job guarantee. Extend working hours, reduce overstaffing, revise salary scales, implement competitive and objective procedures for selecting, evaluating and promotion of public employees that measure performance and reward merit.	●●	LT
INFRASTRUCTURE					
Infrastructure (general)	Deficiencies in the quality and quantity of infrastructure resulting from poor performance of state-owned enterprises and lack of commercial considerations.	●●●	Reassess Government role and implement an agenda of comprehensive policy and institutional change: * permit greater private ownership and management arrangements; * revise the basic legal framework of governance, separating policy-making and regulatory functions of government from operational functions. * implement tariff reform in all public utilities; and * run on commercial basis, with any subsidies provided in a direct and transparent manner.	●●	LT
Telecom	Poor quality of service, especially on local calls. Underinvestment.	●●●	Improve internal management and oversight and broaden scope for private provision, competition.	●●	MT
Roads	Poor quality, with substantial regional variation. Underinvestment.	●●	Improve quality through increased road maintenance. Introduce budgetary reform in MPW to permit sufficient and sustainable financing for road maintenance; permit greater private participation	●●	MT

CONSTRAINTS			RECOMMENDATIONS		
Area	Issues	Priority	Recommendations	Tech. Diffic.	Period of Impl.
INFRASTRUCTURE *(Cont'd)*					
Power	Voltage/frequency fluctuations. Underinvestment	●●●	Complete reforms introduced, grant new concessions for private power generation.	●●	MT
Water	Inadequate supply and regional variations, with disjointed institutional framework.	●	Implement tariff reform, address governance issues, permit private participation, strengthen the project pipeline.	●●	LT
LEGAL AND REGULATORY FRAMEWORK					
Legal, Regulatory and Administrative Issues.	Inadequate protection of real and intellectual property rights.	●●●	Modernize and improve efficiency of Registry of Real Property; upgrade capacity to register and protect intellectual property.	●	MT
	Difficulties for domestic and foreign business entry and operation.	●●	Simplify and harmonize rules and institutional structures.	●	ST
	Inadequate laws and procedures for bankruptcy.	●	Revise laws allowing speedy proceedings and introduce alternatives for defaulting debtors.	●	ST
	Inadequate regulation of competitive behavior and little enforcement of consumer protection law.	●●	Strengthen competition policy and consumer protection by enacting modern competition/ antitrust law, streamlining consumer protection law, creating autonomous enforcement agency.	●●	MT
	Poor functioning and enforcement capacity of judicial system; no alternative dispute resolution mechanisms.	●●●	Set up bar association to regulate legal profession, establish standards for judges, train and inform commercial judge, and facilitate use of alternative dispute resolution mechanisms.	●●●	LT
Tax Rules and Administration	Exemptions and evasions of VAT, income tax combined with uneven enforcement distorts incentives, creates sense of unfairness that undermines business confidence.	●●	Include construction industry, electricity consumption in VAT; tax financial instruments and personal interest income.	●	ST
	Complex procedures and slow and discretionary processing increase private sector compliance costs.	●●	Strengthen capacity; improve information systems, develop strategic audit plan, streamline regulations and procedures, enforce laws uniformly.	●●	MT

CONSTRAINTS			RECOMMENDATIONS		
Area	**Issues**	**Priority**	**Recommendations**	**Tech. Diffic.**	**Period of Impl.**
TRADE AND TECHNOLOGICAL DIFFUSION					
Foreign Trade Regime	Trade policy: high tariff dispersion and trade biases; administrative regulations on imports still exist.	●●	Deepen and sustain trade liberalization by moving to a uniform tariff rate and eliminating remaining administrative instruments regulating import flows.	●	MT
	Import procedures are lengthy, complicated and non-transparent.	●	Establish one stop window for imports; Accelerate on-going customs reforms.	● ●●	ST MT
	Export procedures and institutions suffer from poor service, long procedures, extra costs.	●●●	Accelerate document processing by CENTREX; add user fee to finance new offices away from center.	●	ST
	FTZ and Fiscal Areas Scheme: complicated, non-transparent procedures, discretionary practices in customs.	●	Further streamline FTZ and fiscal areas.	●	ST
	The duty drawback system does not function well and is discriminatory.	●	In the medium-term eliminate the duty drawback. In the interim, improve functioning and eliminate discrimination.	●●	MT
Technological Innovation and Enterprise Development	Lack of access and absorption	●●	Support greater access to foreign technologies through trade, licensing agreements, and FDI. Encourage development of private sector support services and initiatives. Ensure supportive human and physical infrastructure	●●●	MT
Trade Negotiations	Need to seize opportunities to gain access to new markets and market new products.	●	Continue strengthening trade negotiation capabilities.	●●	MT
Government-Business Consultation	Lack of systematic means for businesses to communicate concerns and opportunities to key government agencies and for government to disseminate information on policy and collect information on its economic impact at the firm level.	●●	Establish one or more focused consultative committees of government and business representatives to discuss concrete steps to promote growth-oriented, equitable, market-based reforms.	●●	MT

CONSTRAINTS			RECOMMENDATIONS		
Area	Issues	Priority	Recommendations	Tech. Diffic.	Period of Impl.
FINANCIAL SECTOR					
Access to Credit	Lack of an efficient system to create and enforce collateral security.	●●●	Address collateral security issues by revising the legal framework and improving public registries to ensure effective creation, perfection, and enforcement of security interests.	●●●	MT
	Limited use of new financing instruments (e.g., leasing).	●●	Revise laws and guidelines on use of financing instruments and liens on inventory and commercial equipment.	●	ST
	Limited access by small and micro enterprises	●●●	Try new approaches along the lines of successful experiences (e.g., Grameen Bank, Banco Solidario)	●●●	LT
Banking System: Prudential Regulation and Supervision	Lack of adequate regulatory and prudential framework.	●●●	Strengthen prudential and regulatory system by: (i) developing regulation to decrease illiquidity risks, (ii) establishing deposit insurance fund, (iii) implementing a rating system, strengthening information accounting standards, and developing ongoing training programs.	●●	MT
	Lack of accurate interest rate information.	●	Ensure more accurate interest rate information through periodic Central Bank or SSF publication.	●	ST
Deposit Insurance	Lack of deposit insurance	●●	Accelerate efforts to establish a well functioning deposit insurance fund.	●●	ST
Competition and Bank Ownership	Limitations on ownership restricts competition, raising of new capital and imposes heavy administrative burden.	●●	Eliminate ownership limitations including 5% rule and restrictions on foreign ownership.	●	ST
Capital Market Development	Dearth of potential private sector issuers.	●●	Catalyze supply by: (i) using public issues to establish pricing benchmark and provide liquidity, and (ii) enhancing collaborative efforts with CACM.	●●●	LT
	Insufficient disclosure of financial information and insufficient quality of information on current market trends.	●	Ensure reliable and timely information by: (i) supporting development of risk rating agencies, (ii) encouraging accounting firms to establish a self-regulatory body and (iii) ensuring provision of information on transactions.	●●	MT
	Weak supervision of securities exchange, insurance and pensions.	●●	Strengthen supervision by further developing capabilities of SSF.	●●●	LT
	Lack of financial intermediaries.	●●	Facilitate development of financial intermediaries by developing new legislation for contractual savings institutions (insurance companies and pension funds) and creating enabling legislation for mutual funds and leasing companies.	●●●	LT

ADDENDUM

During the finalization of this report, the Central Bank developed a new system of national accounts, including rebasing from 1962 to 1990 prices. The tables and figures included in the text of this report reflect data at 1962 prices, since overall economic trends remain unchanged with the rebasing. This addendum highlights methodological changes and major differences between the two data sets.

The national accounts were rebased because 1962 prices no longer reflected current economic behavior as the production structure has undergone substantial qualitative changes. In 1962, coffee had a predominant weight in the economy, petroleum prices were low, inflation was non-existent, and consumption patterns and the tax structure were markedly different. The new system of national accounts introduced the following methodological changes:

⇨ the valuation of exports and imports of goods and non-factor services was modified using market exchange rates to convert from US dollars to colones;
⇨ the composition of GDP by sector of origin was modified by methodological changes in the valuation of the financial sector, of net subsidies, and of import duties; and
⇨ the value added of productive activities was affected by changes in the treatment of the different stages of production; adjustments for seasonal activities in agriculture; and changes in the calculation of production credited to the financial sector and commerce.

The main data implications of the new system of national accounts are:

⇨ nominal GDP is lower by approximately 10 percent in 1993 and 8 percent in 1994;
⇨ real GDP growth is higher: 7.5, 7.4, and 6.0 percent in 1992, 1993, and 1994, respectively, at 1990 prices, compared with 5.3, 5.1 and 5.8 for those same years at 1962 prices;
⇨ the contribution of the primary sector to GDP is higher, the contribution of secondary production is approximately the same, and the contribution of the service sector is lower, although it remains the most important sector;
⇨ exports and imports as percentage of GDP are higher, reaching 20 and 35 percent, respectively, in 1994, compared with 13 and 27 percent in the previous data set; however, resource balances are approximately the same with the two data sets during the 1990s; and
⇨ gross domestic expenditure as percentage of GDP is approximately the same in the two data sets, although consumption is slightly lower and investment is higher, reaching 18.8 percent of GDP in 1994, compared with 17.8 percent in the previous data set.

CHAPTER I

ENTERING A NEW STAGE OF DEVELOPMENT: CHALLENGES AND OPPORTUNITIES

"Our vision as a nation is to transform El Salvador into a land of opportunities, with equity....We want to make the country attractive to national and foreign investment, and incorporate ourselves into the world production chain....El Salvador has a magnificent opportunity to make a great leap forward in quality. We either enter the process of globalization now, or other countries will do it. We either are among the first, or we get there at the end, to take what is left in the world market....The country demands a modern, efficient, and competitive private sector, who in turn demands a modern and efficient public sector capable of creating an enabling environment for private sector development." (Excerpts from a speech by President Calderón Sol on February 2, 1995).

This chapter summarizes achievements since 1989; presents the main features of the new development strategy aiming at accelerating equitable growth by enhancing global competitiveness; identifies the necessary conditions to achieve this vision; and summarizes the key features of the public-private sector interaction. It concludes that the necessary conditions to successfully implement the new development strategy include: higher investment and savings; greater levels and quality of human capital; enhanced allocative efficiency and productivity growth; and higher exports. In parallel to public sector modernization, the challenge is to remove existing constraints to outward-oriented private sector-led growth.

ECONOMIC AND POLITICAL ACHIEVEMENTS: 1989-94

Since 1989, El Salvador's policy makers have accomplished three remarkable achievements: end the civil war; implement a coherent economic strategy leading to the stabilization of the economy and the reactivation of growth; and initiate a systematic attack on poverty. These efforts have lifted the country from the economic crisis of the 1980s and have led it to a path of relative stability and economic growth, compared to other developing countries. In June 1989 the authorities initiated the implementation of a comprehensive economic stabilization and adjustment program. As the adjustment program took hold and peace prospects improved, the economy stabilized and began to recover. The country's economic performance during the past six years is a remarkable success story. During the 1990s, El Salvador has registered among the highest growth rates in the hemisphere and this has occurred despite the migration of the best of its labor force to the United States (Table I-1).

THE NEW DEVELOPMENT STRATEGY: GOALS AND GENESIS

The objective of the bold economic reforms presented by President Calderón Sol on February 2, 1995, is to achieve more rapid and equitable growth by enhancing global competitiveness. The aim is for El Salvador to enter the 21st century as a more open and equitable economy. The two main intermediate economic goals are to rapidly: (i) promote domestic and foreign investment and incorporate the country into the global production chain by lowering the costs of operating in the country; and (ii) reduce the size of the State through accelerated privatization, while strengthening the public sector's role as facilitator of private sector development. The Government has announced actions in four main policy areas:

⇨ *accelerating trade liberalization*;
⇨ *modernizing the public sector*, focusing on six areas: decentralization, regulatory framework, privatization, civil service reform, reform of the pension system, and procurement;
⇨ *strengthening fiscal discipline* by increasing revenue collection and rationalizing expenditures; and
⇨ *maintaining nominal exchange rate stability and allowing voluntary dollarization.*

Table I.1 Key Macroeconomic Indicators, 1980-95

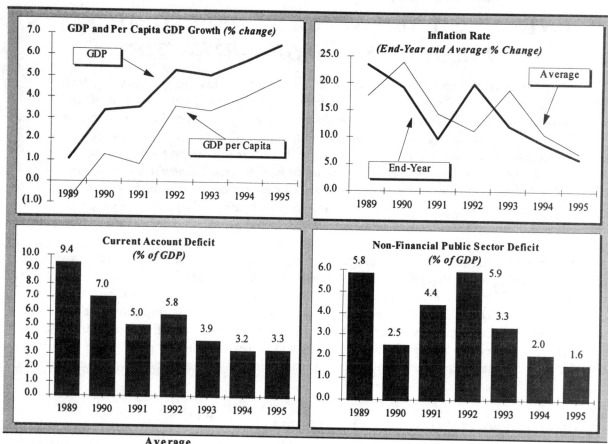

	Average						Proj.
	1980-88	**1989**	**1990**	**1991**	**1992**	**1993**	**1994**	**1995**
National Accounts (as % of GDP)								
Gross Investment	13.2	15.3	11.8	13.8	16.1	16.6	17.8	19.7
Public	4.7	3.5	2.3	2.5	3.6	3.6	3.5	4.0
Private	8.5	11.8	9.5	11.3	12.4	13.0	14.3	15.7
Gross National Savings	8.7	5.9	4.8	8.8	10.3	12.7	14.6	16.4
Public	0.4	(1.6)	(0.3)	(0.7)	0.2	0.7	1.9	3.1
Private	8.2	7.5	5.1	9.5	10.1	12.0	12.7	13.3
Foreign Savings a/	4.6	9.4	7.0	5.0	5.8	3.9	3.2	3.3
Non-Financial Public Sector (as % of GDP)								
Current Revenues a/	16.1	10.3	11.1	11.6	12.3	12.5	14.5	16.5
o/w Tax Revenues	11.1	7.6	8.1	8.5	8.7	9.4	10.5	11.5
Current Expenditures	15.7	11.8	11.4	12.3	12.1	11.8	12.6	13.4
Public Savings	0.4	(1.6)	(0.3)	(0.7)	0.2	0.7	1.9	3.1
Overall Balance a/	(7.2)	(5.8)	(2.5)	(4.4)	(5.9)	(3.3)	(2.0)	(1.6)
Balance of Payments (as % of GDP)								
Exports of GNFS	24.8	15.4	16.8	14.9	13.6	14.0	13.4	-
Imports of GNFS	29.8	27.5	28.6	27.3	29.2	28.1	27.4	-
Trade Balance	(5.1)	(13.4)	(13.3)	(13.8)	(16.8)	(15.5)	(15.0)	(15.7)
Remittances	2.8	4.8	6.8	9.2	10.8	10.8	10.7	10.8
Current Account Balance	(4.6)	(9.4)	(7.0)	(5.0)	(5.8)	(3.9)	(3.2)	(3.3)
Overall Balance	0.1	(0.7)	1.8	(0.9)	(0.3)	2.0	1.5	1.9
Bilat. Real Exch. Rate b/	134.7	93.8	107.3	110.0	103.7	92.4	88.2	-
Creditworthiness Indicators								
Total DOD/GDP	39.9	41.9	42.0	36.8	34.4	26.4	-	-
Total DOD/Exports G&S	161.4	258.8	237.1	234.4	234.0	172.1	-	-
Total Debt Service/Expor	19.3	26.9	23.0	26.7	24.8	26.0	-	-

Note: Based on 1962 prices.   a/ Excluding grants and Central Bank losses.   b/ Index 1985=100.
Sources: Central Reserve Bank of El Salvador and World Bank Debt Tables.

Notwithstanding the achievements of the 1989-94 period, three main considerations led the Government to reassess the country's development strategy:

⇨ **The need for more rapid growth**. More rapid economic growth is a necessary condition to alleviate poverty and consolidate peace. Although growth improved in the post-war period, GDP per capita remains at pre-war levels and the trickle down effects of prosperity have not yet been felt widely enough. Real GDP levels are only approximately equal to those of the late 1970s and GDP per capita in 1994 was still below 1970 levels (Figure I.1).

⇨ **Growth sustainability concerns.** El Salvador's pattern of growth in recent years presents some risks: (i) increasing reliance on the non-tradable sector; recent relatively high growth rates have been associated with a service and construction boom (Table I.2) spurred by repressed demand during the war and high remittances; and (ii) extremely low export levels (Figure I.2).

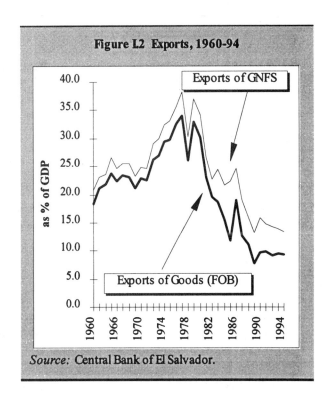

Figure I.1 GDP and GDP per Capita, 1960-94 (in 1990 Colones)

Sources: IMF, IFS and Central Bank of El Salvador.

Table I.2 Sectoral GDP Shares and Growth Rates

Period 1975-94	Prim.	Secondary			Serv.
		Manuf.	Const.	Pub. U.	
GDP Shares (percent)					
1975-94	19.3	16.9	3.4	2.1	58.4
1975-78	27.7	16.2	4.3	1.5	50.2
1979-91	19.0	16.6	3.1	2.2	59.2
1992-94	9.2	19.0	3.1	2.5	66.2
Sectoral Growth Rate (average)					
1975-94	1.0	1.8	4.0	5.5	1.5
1975-78	3.9	5.8	17.3	10.8	5.5
1979-91	-0.6	-0.7	-1.6	2.8	-0.4
1992-94	4.2	7.2	10.5	9.9	4.5
Contribution to GDP Growth Rate					
1975-94	0.1	0.4	0.2	0.1	0.9
1975-78	1.2	1.0	0.8	0.2	2.8
1979-91	-0.2	-0.1	-0.1	0.1	-0.1
1992-94	0.4	1.4	0.3	0.2	3.0

Note: Primary=agric.and mining; Serv.=commerce, banking, & housing. *Source:* Central Bank of El Salvador.

Figure I.2 Exports, 1960-94

Source: Central Bank of El Salvador.

⇨ **The challenge of globalization.** Globalization - driven by widespread adoption of liberalization policies, buoyant world trade, technological catching up, increasing capital flows, and the internationalization of services - represents a fundamental opportunity for raising welfare in both developing and industrial economies (World Bank 1995). However, recent trends in international economic integration also highlight the need for developing countries to move away from narrow dependence on commodity exports and become globally competitive in technologically more advanced goods and services. To benefit from the new opportunities in trade and finance, developing economies must: (i) transform policies and structures to support outward-oriented growth; (ii) move resources toward more knowledge-intensive goods and services to take advantage of shifting relative prices and expanding boundaries of tradability; (iii) acquire high technology by plugging into the world economy and by attracting foreign investment; and (iv) ensure adequate human and physical infrastructure, since they are more important than low wages in attracting investment.

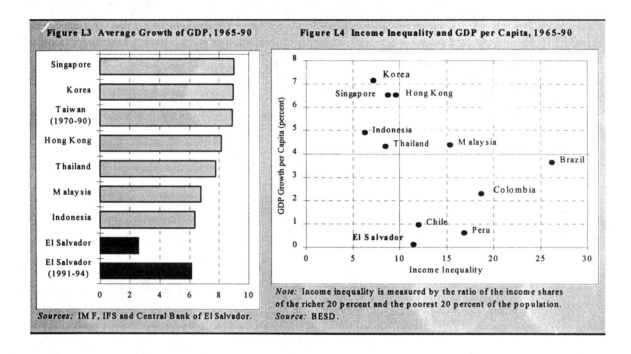

Figure I.3 Average Growth of GDP, 1965-90

Figure I.4 Income Inequality and GDP per Capita, 1965-90

Sources: IMF, IFS and Central Bank of El Salvador.

Note: Income inequality is measured by the ratio of the income shares of the richer 20 percent and the poorest 20 percent of the population.
Source: BESD.

LESSONS FROM EAST ASIA

The Salvadoran authorities have been looking at East Asia as an example of a successful development model characterized by rapid and equitable growth (Figures I.3 and I.4), although they have distanced themselves from interventionist public policies. The comparison with East Asian economies suggests that to accelerate growth in El Salvador, the focus should be on augmenting physical and human resource accumulation, enhancing the allocative efficiency and the productivity of resources, and increasing outward orientation.

⇨ **Low investment and savings levels.** The East Asian economies have higher growth of physical capital and higher national savings. Notwithstanding improvements during the last four years, El Salvador continues to show relatively low investment and savings levels (Figures I.5a and I.5b). Low investment levels are due to the impact of the civil war and a very regulated and distortionary macroeconomic environment during the 1980s, and to existing constraints to private sector development which increase the costs and the risks of doing business. Although worker remittances have increased national savings, continued low domestic savings levels reflect inadequate public savings, the increase in private consumption fueled by remittances, and the lack of opportunities for financial savings.

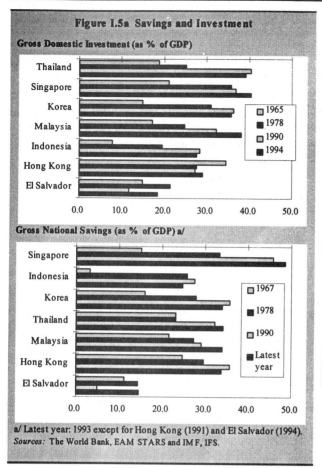

Figure I.5a Savings and Investment

Gross Domestic Investment (as % of GDP)

Gross National Savings (as % of GDP) a/

a/ Latest year: 1993 except for Hong Kong (1991) and El Salvador (1994).
Sources: The World Bank, EAM STARS and IMF, IFS.

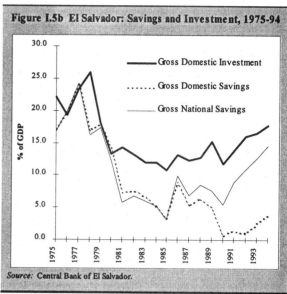

Figure I.5b El Salvador: Savings and Investment, 1975-94

Source: Central Bank of El Salvador.

⇨ **Inadequate human capital.** The East Asian economies showed higher initial levels and growth rates of human capital. El Salvador is currently characterized by: (i) a low human capital stock (Figure I.6a); (ii) low primary enrollment ratios which do not bode well for a rapid increase in the stock (Figure I.6b); and (iii) low educational quality exemplified by high repetition and dropout rates. These constraints are critical given the Government's goal of moving toward a more technologically and outward-oriented strategy, which requires an educated and flexible labor force. The Government has been accelerating efforts to address these constraints to counter domestic pressures to slow down the opening up of the economy.

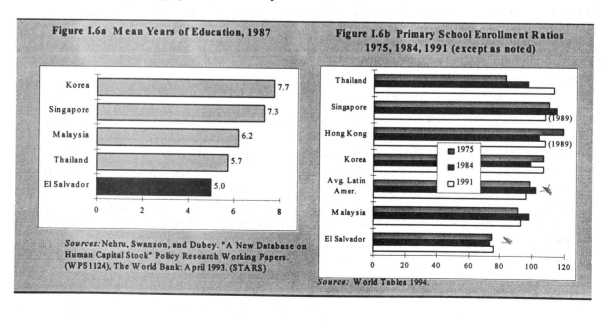

Figure I.6a Mean Years of Education, 1987

Sources: Nehru, Swanson, and Dubey. "A New Database on Human Capital Stock" Policy Research Working Papers. (WPS1124), The World Bank: April 1993. (STARS)

Figure I.6b Primary School Enrollment Ratios
1975, 1984, 1991 (except as noted)

Source: World Tables 1994.

⇨ **Low allocation efficiency and productivity growth.** While two-thirds of East Asia's growth is due to rapid physical and human capital accumulation, the remaining third is attributed to total factor productivity (TFP) growth.[1]

Table I.3 El Salvador: Sources of Growth

Period	Growth of			Average	Absolute contribution to growth		
	GDPpr	K	L	L share	K	L	TFP
60-90	2.56	5.53	2.36	0.45	3.05	1.08	-1.53
60-73	5.24	6.57	3.14	0.53	3.09	1.66	0.49
73-90	0.00	4.05	1.71	0.39	2.49	0.66	-3.14

Source: V. Nehru and A. Dhaneshawar (June 1994); staff estimates.

Estimates of the determinants of economic growth[2] for El Salvador based on work by Nehru and Dhareshwar (1994) suggest: (i) a negative TFP contribution (i.e., overall inefficiencies) for 1960-90, which exceeded increases in output attributed to labor; (ii) overall inef-ficiencies (low or negative TFP) fared worse during the second period, which included the war years; and (iii) during 1960-73, when TFP was positive, its relative contribution to growth was approximately 10 percent.

TFP growth in East Asian countries has been much larger than in El Salvador (Table I.4). The main sources of high TFP growth in East Asia are: (i) efficient resource allocation, through market mechanisms, in the labor market, the capital market, and international trade; and (ii) techno-logical catching-up accompanied by high and rising levels of human capital which ensured effective use of new technologies.

Table I.4 Total Factor Productivity (TFP) Growth, 1960-90 (%)

| Country | EAM 1960-90 | Nehru and Dhareshwar | | | | | |
| | | 1960-90 | | 1960-72 | | 1972-90 | |
		A	B	A	B	A	B
El Salvador	-	-1.53	-0.58	1.51	2.42	-2.31	-1.46
Taiwan	3.76	0.41	2.21	4.39	7.08	2.61	2.60
Hong Kong	3.64	-	-	-	-	-	-
Korea	3.10	0.71	2.43	4.16	5.65	2.90	3.38
Thailand	2.50	0.09	1.73	3.15	4.81	1.90	2.56
Indonesia	1.25	0.19	1.05	1.77	2.24	0.70	1.30
Singapore	1.19	-0.61	1.22	3.67	6.47	1.50	1.92
Malaysia	1.08	-0.18	1.11	1.98	3.60	0.95	1.69

A: level regression, using an error-correction model considered by the authors more appropriate for capturing long-term relations from the data.
B: using first difference regressions.
Source: World Bank, 1993, 64; and Nehru and Dhareshwar, 1994.

⇨ **Low exports and outward orientation.** Table I.5 highlights the dramatic decline in exports and trade ratios since 1980. In 1994 exports of goods increased to almost 10 percent of GDP - reaching 15 percent of GDP if "maquila" exports are included - thanks to macroeconomic stability and accelerated trade liberalization. Notwithstanding recent improvements, the attainment of much higher export levels and a more diversified export base are critical for the achievement of the Government's goal of accelerating growth.

Table I.5 Ratio of Total Trade to GDP

| Country | Exports of Goods/GDP | | | (Exports+Imports)/GDP | | |
	1970	1980	1992	1970	1980	1992
Singapore	83	162	135	214	363	289
Hong Kong	56	50	31	137	130	159
Malaysia	40	53	70	74	97	138
Thailand	10	20	29	28	49	66
Korea	9	28	25	32	63	51
Indonesia	11	28	27	21	42	48
El Salvador	22	20	8	43	48	32

Sources: The World Bank, World Tables 1994.

---

[1] TFP is the variation in output not explained by input changes and measures the efficiency with which inputs are used (i.e., changes in output per unit of all inputs combined). Increases in TFP may result from improved resource allocation, economies of scale, innovation, absorption of new technologies, gains from specialization, and in general any factors reducing real production costs (World Bank 1991 and 1993).
[2] Empirical estimates of source sof growth provide a simplified framework to analyze the contribution to economic growth (GDPgr) of accumulation of factor inputs (capital [K] and labor [L] amd TFP growth.

THE PUBLIC-PRIVATE SECTOR INTERACTION: POLICY IMPLICATIONS

The return to peace, the existence of a comprehensive long-term economic strategy, and changes in the global economic environment have created the opportunities for the attainment of El Salvador's vision. Key constraints to meeting the challenge of globalization are not economic distortions or excessive government activity and regulation, per se. Instead, they lie in weak support systems for private enterprises that inhibit productivity growth and international competitiveness. Public sector modernization and private sector development are two sides of the same coin, and their interaction and complementarity are critical. To accelerate growth, the Government should continue removing existing constraints to outward-orientation and private sector growth, productivity, and competitiveness by reforming the State and, in parallel, implementing a comprehensive private sector development strategy.

Key constraints. The share of the public sector in GDP and investment, and the regulatory framework are not excessive by international standards. The main constraints are related to weak support systems for private enterprises. As identified in the Enterprise Survey these include:

⇨ **Inefficiencies and underinvestment in infrastructure, education, and health: the State as owner and operator**. Deficiencies in infrastructure services severely inhibit international competitiveness. Innovation in Salvadoran industry is likely to be slow unless there is a significant increase in foreign investment. That, in turn, will not come if physical infrastructure is inadequate for businesses operating in international markets. In addition, inefficiencies in social sector services have led to inadequate levels and productivity of human capital.

⇨ **Human and financial resource management weaknesses: the State as administrator.** A key problem underlying the poor quality and inefficiency of public sector human resources is the lack of an effective management structure and process. In addition, financial management issues exist in: expenditure planning, budget preparation, and resource allocation; treasury and payments systems; budget execution; auditing; and responsibility and accountability incentives and procedures. These weaknesses have a direct impact on the capacity of the State to: (i) ensure a stable macroeconomic environment; (ii) ensure social peace and political stability; and (iii) foster a meritocratic and politically independent bureaucracy.

⇨ **Constraints related to the formulation, implementation, and enforcement of rules and regulations in the business environment and the financial sector: the State as regulator.** Distortions and inflexibilities exist in the legal and regulatory framework, labor markets, financial sector rules and supervision, and trade and export development policies.

Public sector modernization. The State should reform itself to ensure efficient provision of essential public goods and services and to reorient public resources to support economic growth and attend to the most urgent needs of the poor. Key areas will be: (i) increasing private participation in the provision of public services, through privatization, contracting out of service delivery, and decentralization; (ii) improving the quality, efficiency, and coverage of the public services which the State will continue to provide; and (iii) strengthening the policy-making and management capacity of the public sector. To this end, the Government is implementing a comprehensive Public Sector Modernization Program supported by bilateral and multilateral donors. Its full and timely implementation is the necessary condition for entering the new stage of development.

Private sector development. In parallel, the Government is developing a policy agenda to support the private sector, which already plays a predominant role in the economy. With the privatization of the financial sector, the dismantling of state agricultural marketing, and the offering for sale of most state-owned productive assets, the private sector now produces over 90 percent of GDP and accounts for about

93 percent of total employment. To remove existing constraints to the acceleration of outward-oriented private sector-led growth the Government should act rapidly and concurrently on six fundamental policy areas: (i) further enhancing the stability of the macroeconomic framework; (ii) developing human resources and increasing labor productivity and flexibility; (iii) modernizing infrastructure; (iv) improving the legal and regulatory framework; (v) facilitating trade and technological diffusion; and (vi) strengthening the financial sector.

CHAPTER II

ENHANCING MACROECONOMIC STABILITY

This chapter assesses the need for further macroeconomic adjustment within the framework of the Government's new development strategy. It analyzes constraints and proposes a policy agenda to improve fiscal performance and to address macroeconomic management issues related to high and sustained foreign exchange flows. It concludes that to successfully meet the challenge of globalization and accelerate growth further macroeconomic adjustment is needed. In an increasingly more open, integrated, and competitive global economy, economic management must ensure stability to maintain the confidence of domestic and international markets, and flexibly respond to more mobile and potentially volatile cross-border capital flows. El Salvador has shown remarkable macroeconomic improvements since 1989 but the Government should continue implementing polices to:

⇨ further improve fiscal performance;
⇨ relieve inflationary and interest rate pressures;
⇨ ensure a credible exchange rate policy; and
⇨ address external viability concerns.

To improve fiscal performance, the tax base should be broadened, compliance enforced, and the on-going public sector modernization program should be fully and timely implemented. To address macroeconomic management issues related to capital inflows, in the long-run, the challenge is to adjust to the higher level of foreign exchange inflows. This can be achieved by implementing policies which, in addition to improving fiscal performance, should aim at encouraging high levels of savings and investment and further trade liberalization, and at pursuing a credible exchange rate policy while limiting real exchange rate appreciation. Finally, to ensure external sector viability, the Government should facilitate private sector efforts to increase productivity and global competitiveness and expand and diversify the export base within a framework of a lower real exchange rate.

IMPROVING FISCAL PERFORMANCE

Improvements in fiscal performance since 1989 are fragile because of low public savings, low capital expenditures, inertial and inflexible expenditure patterns, and dependence on external financing. Within on-going efforts to reform the public sector, two priority areas must be addressed:

✓ increasing tax revenues to increase public savings and decrease reliance on external financing; and
✓ modernizing the public sector to improve efficiency.

Fragility of fiscal performance

El Salvador's fiscal deficits are decreasing and total public expenditures are not excessive (Figure II.1). However, much remains to be done in four areas:

⇨ *increase public savings*, mostly through a greater tax effort while increasing the efficiency of expenditures (Figure II.2);
⇨ *avoid relying on lowering capital expenditures to ensure fiscal improvements*, a trend which has constrained public investment in social sectors and infrastructure (Figures II.3 and II.4);
⇨ *address inertial and inflexible expenditure patterns*, resulting from a relatively high share of spending on wages and salaries (which averaged 55 percent of current expenditures over the past four

years) and serious rigidities and deficiencies in financial and human resource management. The success of the Government's development strategy depends on an efficient reorientation of resources toward priority areas, such as social sectors and infrastructure, and away from wages and salaries;

⇨ *and improve fiscal performance to limit financing vulnerability issues*; deficits are being financed exclusively through foreign sources,[1] limiting the inflationary impact of the deficits but further complicating monetary management of foreign exchange inflows and increasing the vulnerability to external shocks.

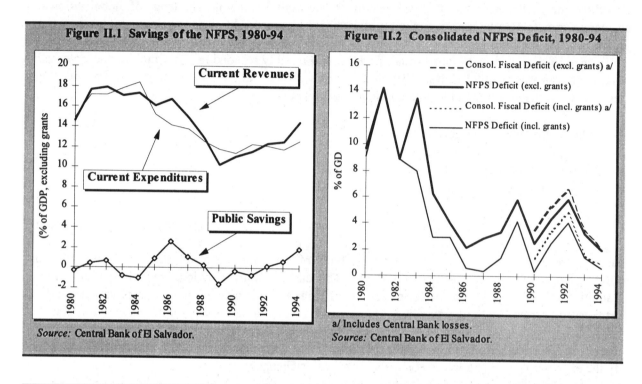

Figure II.1 Savings of the NFPS, 1980-94

Source: Central Bank of El Salvador.

Figure II.2 Consolidated NFPS Deficit, 1980-94

a/ Includes Central Bank losses.
Source: Central Bank of El Salvador.

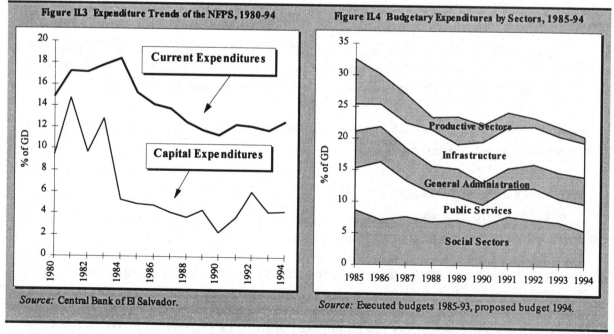

Figure II.3 Expenditure Trends of the NFPS, 1980-94

Source: Central Bank of El Salvador.

Figure II.4 Budgetary Expenditures by Sectors, 1985-94

Source: Executed budgets 1985-93, proposed budget 1994.

---

[1] Since 1991, legislation has banned Central Bank lending to the Government to finance public sector deficits. A proposal to include this prohibition in the Constitution is currently under discussion.

Increasing revenues

Tax revenues accounted for 10.5 percent of GDP in 1994 (Figure II.5), well below international standards, although expenditures were also below international averages. The tax base currently relies on a 13 percent value added tax (VAT, accounting for over 40 percent of tax revenues), income taxes (27 percent), and trade taxes (18.3 percent).

Although reforms implemented since 1990 have increased revenues and produced a more efficient and equitable tax system, they have not raised sufficiently its revenue generating capacity and its buoyancy. If the public sector deficit is to be reduced, while providing a reasonable level of essential services, reforms must raise the country's tax effort beyond the levels it had reached in the mid-1980s (12-13 percent of GDP).

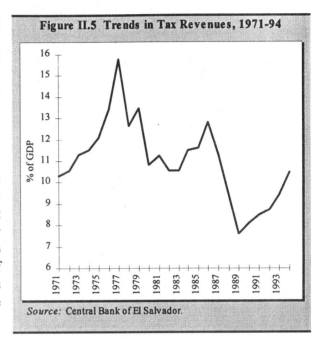

Figure II.5 Trends in Tax Revenues, 1971-94

Source: Central Bank of El Salvador.

Key constraints are a narrow tax base and weak administration. Structural and exogenous factors, such as the land tenure pattern, the large number of small establishments, the armed conflict, and falling coffee prices contributed to the erosion of the tax base. To raise the revenue generating capacity of its tax system to at least 14 percent of GDP per year by the end of the century, the Government should consider: (i) further steps to broaden the tax base; and (ii) improving tax administration to significantly increase compliance and reduce evasion.

Broadening the tax base

The low tax effort can be partly explained by the narrow coverage of some taxes resulting from exclusions, generous deductions, exemptions, fraudulent non-compliance, and non-reporting. The tax reform of 1992 has done away with some of the limitations, but has not broadened the tax base sufficiently. The repeal of the net wealth tax in April 1994 narrowed the tax base even further. Areas where there is scope for broadening the tax base include:

⇨ **Eliminate VAT exemptions** in: (i) the construction industry where only contractual work involving alterations, repairs, and maintenance is subject to VAT; (ii) financial services; and (iii) public utilities (electricity, water, and sewerage). These exemptions narrow the base and generate distortions, since exempt items and sectors cannot claim credit for VAT paid on input purchases. The feasibility of incorporating the entirety of the construction industry needs to be evaluated, but new construction should be subject to the VAT. Although equity and efficiency arguments favor the taxation of financial instruments under the VAT, their inclusion would create difficulties. Hence, it would be preferable to tax them separately under a stamp duty or registration fees to fill the gap created by repeal of the stamp tax. In the public utilities the sales-to-purchase ratio is quite high while the debit-to-credit ratio is very low. This suggests that their incorporation into the VAT could yield substantial additional revenue.

⇨ **Limit high personal income tax exemptions and deductions**, especially since the personal income tax is levied on individual persons and not on families. The 1992 reform left a large majority of wage and salary earners and a large number of unincorporated enterprises outside the tax net.

⇨ **Incorporate the interest income received by individuals into the personal income tax base**. Currently, dividends are taxable under the income tax; so is interest income received by businesses, but not interest income received by individuals from their deposits in banks and other financial institutions.

⇨ **Introduce presumptive methods in taxing incomes,**[2] not only to raise revenue, but also to enhance equity and efficiency. Presumptive methods are an administratively convenient way to collect taxes from hard-to-tax groups. Since wages and salaries are taxed much more effectively than incomes of the self-employed, presumptive methods of taxing professionals (e.g., by establishing minima for different categories), broaden the base, improve horizontal equity, and enhance efficiency. Application of the profit margin of small taxpayers to all taxpayers in a given category to assess their income could encourage enterprises to increase their efficiency, since any surplus would have a marginal rate of zero.

⇨ **Extend to VAT the applicability of presumptive methods of taxation**, as is done in many countries.[3] This requires the development of guidelines for various economic activities based on careful studies of particular trades, industries, and professions.

⇨ **Revise motor vehicle registration fees** to reflect purchase values or revise specific fees frequently.

Strengthening tax administration and enforcing compliance

Improving tax and customs administration, enforcing compliance, and ensuring that taxes are assessed and collected correctly should be key policy objectives. Unless compliance is raised considerably, tax reforms will have limited impact. Notwithstanding initiation of a comprehensive tax and customs administration program supported by USAID, IDB, and the World Bank, tax administration is still deficient in assessing, collecting, and enforcing compliance. While fully implementing the on-going reform program, the Government should:

⇨ **Implement an efficient tax penalty system** by improving the effectiveness of the *Ley del Delito Fiscal* which has been hampered by: imprecise definitions of punishable fiscal crimes; lack of harmonization with VAT and Income Tax Laws; and lengthy procedures.

⇨ **Make examples of tax evaders**. Large VAT payers (businesses with annual sales exceeding 36 million colones) represent a mere 0.5 percent of the universe, but account for 60 percent of total sales and 48 percent of the total VAT collected. Similarly, according to unaudited tax returns, corporate income taxpayers in the highest net taxable profit group represent only 1.1 percent of the universe, but account for 60 percent of total taxable profits and 63 percent of the corporate tax yield.

⇨ **Intensify efforts to improve border controls and customs administration** to reduce corruption and smuggling. Smuggling is particularly rampant in cigarettes, alcoholic beverages, shoes, apparel, textiles, and electronic equipment. Privatizating customs operations should be considered.

⇨ **Intensify efforts to improve income tax administration** by training staff to enforce tax rules and strengthen the system of collecting due taxes. Information systems are inadequate, personnel are not sufficiently trained and coordination between tax administration units is weak.

⇨ **Improve the auditing capacity of the Ministry of Finance,** especially for VAT collection, and enforce strict auditing to prevent evasion by small and micro enterprises and possible bookkeeping mismanagement by large taxpayers. The Government should intensify on-going efforts to improve strategic audit planning by issuing audit manuals and uniformly applying auditing techniques and procedures.

---

[2] This is a common practice in many countries, such as Chile, Colombia, Mexico, Honduras, and Costa Rica.
[3] More than half of the countries that levy a VAT also use presumptive assessment methods to cover firms that are too small to be treated as regular taxpayers, yet large enough not to be exempted.

Modernizing the public sector

Although the room for further expenditure reduction is limited by the need to address large unmet social needs and a relatively low level of expenditures, efficiency gains are possible by: (i) containing current expenditure increases; (ii) reallocating public resources to priority investments, particularly the social sectors and infrastructure; and (iii) improving expenditure management and increasing the efficiency of public investment. The Government can generate these substantial efficiency gains through full and timely implementation of the on-going Public Sector Modernization Program (PSMP). Although the Program is comprehensive, there have been delays in setting up the institutional framework for timely implementation, and in the privatization and civil service reform components.

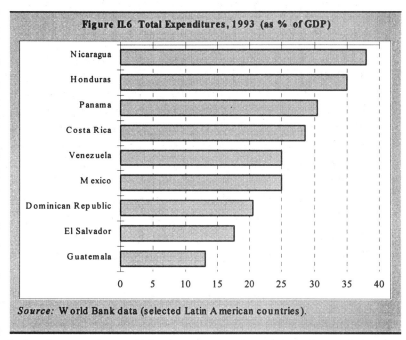

Figure II.6 Total Expenditures, 1993 (as % of GDP)

Source: World Bank data (selected Latin American countries).

ADJUSTING TO HIGH FOREIGN EXCHANGE FLOWS

Notwithstanding their positive impact on living standards and on the balance of payments, high foreign exchange inflows have complicated macroeconomic management and the attainment of other policy fundamentals. In particular, large foreign exchange flows have contributed to inflationary pressures and to the equilibrium appreciation of the real exchange rate. Sterilization policies - to contain monetary expansion and maintain a stable nominal exchange rate - have further complicated macroeconomic management by putting pressure on interest rates and on the Central Bank's operational deficit. In addition, high inflows have contributed to external sector vulnerability.

The high level of foreign exchange flows appears to be permanent in nature although the flows should stabilize at lower growth rates. This entails a change in the underlying structure of the economy. While, in the short-run, the Government should continue open market operations to sterilize excess inflows, these have a limited impact and impose costs in the financial system. In the long-run, the challenge is to adjust to the higher level of inflows by continuing implementation of policies which, in addition to improving fiscal performance, aim at:

✓ raising national savings;

✓ containing inflationary pressures;

✓ pursuing a credible exchange rate policy while limiting real exchange rate appreciation; and

✓ facilitating expansion and diversification of exports, within a framework of a lower real exchange rate.

Background: foreign exchange flows and Dutch disease

Foreign exchange flows: characteristics and trends

High foreign exchange flows are a key contributing factor to current macroeconomic management issues. It is important to summarize trends and characteristics of these flows because a consensus has emerged in the literature that the appropriate policy response depends in great part on their sources and permanence (Calvo, Leiderman, and Reinhart, 1993; and van Wijnbergen, 1984). El Salvador is characterized by: (i) high levels of inflows; (ii) large percentage of remittances which are mostly spent on non-tradable goods; and (iii) prospects for continued total flows in the order of 10 percent of GDP per year.

Since the early 1980s, there have been large increases in net foreign exchange flows, which accelerated after 1989, and again after 1991 as a result of the Peace Accords and reactivation of the economy (Figure II.7). Higher flows are largely due to increasing worker remittances, while capital inflows (excluding remittances) have showed greater variability (Figure II.8). Total inflows or net foreign exchange flows include official transfers, official medium and long term debt flows, private capital,[4] and worker remittances. In addition, high coffee export receipts also contributed to the increase in the supply of foreign exchange during 1994.

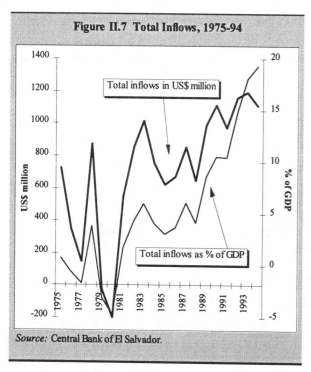

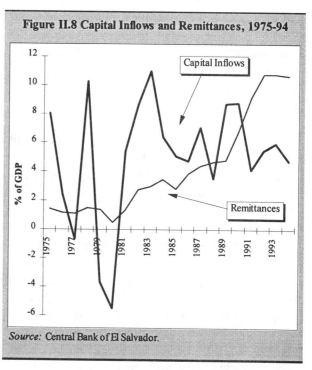

Worker remittances have increased faster than any other inflow and currently represent approximately 70 percent of total foreign exchange flows, while official transfers represent about 20 percent (Figure II.9). Remittances began increasing in the early 1980s as a number of Salvadorans emigrated to the US to escape the civil war (Figures II.10 and II.11). It is estimated that almost 20 percent of the population currently resides abroad, and about 84 percent in the US (FUSADES 1994). It is only in the 1990s that remittances have reached very high levels, but this has been due less to an **actual** increase in remittances than to an increase in **recorded** remittances, as a consequence of the legalization of the parallel foreign exchange market in 1991.

---

[4] Including foreign direct investment (FDI) and private short, medium, and long-term capital flows.

Inflows have relaxed the foreign exchange constraint and have led to international reserve accumulation. In particular, remittances have significantly raised national income and national savings (Table II.1). They have allowed increases in private consumption, which have cushioned the fall in real wages and have had a favorable impact on the balance of payments (akin to increased exports of labor in this case). Estimates show that, on average, over 70 percent of remittances are consumed, mostly in non-tradable goods (FUSADES 1994; and MIPLAN, 1993),

Official transfers and official medium and long term capital have originated in great part from the US and multilateral financial organizations, respectively. These have greatly limited the inflationary impact of fiscal deficits, especially since 1990, and contributed to the consolidation of peace by financing peace-related expenditures.

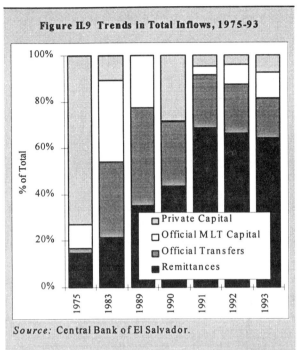

Figure II.9 Trends in Total Inflows, 1975-93

Legend:
- Private Capital
- Official MLT Capital
- Official Transfers
- Remittances

Source: Central Bank of El Salvador.

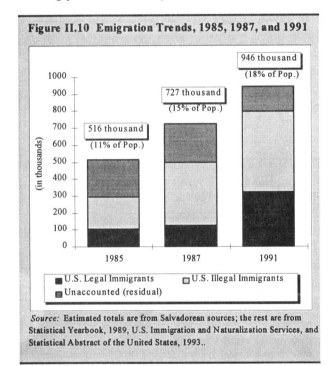

Figure II.10 Emigration Trends, 1985, 1987, and 1991

946 thousand (18% of Pop.)
727 thousand (15% of Pop.)
516 thousand (11% of Pop.)

Legend:
- U.S. Legal Immigrants
- U.S. Illegal Immigrants
- Unaccounted (residual)

Source: Estimated totals are from Salvadorean sources; the rest are from Statistical Yearbook, 1989, U.S. Immigration and Naturalization Services, and Statistical Abstract of the United States, 1993..

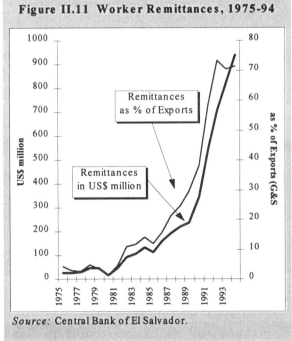

Figure II.11 Worker Remittances, 1975-94

Remittances as % of Exports

Remittances in US$ million

Source: Central Bank of El Salvador.

Table II.1 Remittances and National Income Accounting, 1975-94 (as % of National Income)

	1975-79	1980-88	1989	1990	1991	1992	1993	1994
National Savings	19.4	7.6	5.8	4.6	8.2	9.4	11.5	13.2
Gross Domestic Savings a/	19.6	7.0	3.1	0.1	1.3	0.4	2.2	3.4
Net Factor Income	-1.5	-2.9	-2.0	-1.9	-1.6	-0.8	-0.5	0.1
Remittances	1.3	3.4	4.6	6.4	8.5	9.8	9.8	9.7
Remittances as % of National Savings	6.7	45.1	80.6	140.3	104.1	104.4	85.0	73.2

a/ Data may differ from data in Table 2.7 due to inconsistencies between National Accounts and Balance of Payments.
Source: Central Bank of El Salvador.

Permanence of flows. Inflows are likely to continue at high levels - in the order of 10 percent of GDP - at least during the next 5 years:

⇨ *Remittances.* As long as emigrant workers remain in the US, and the US economy continues growing, remittances will continue. However, they should not increase much beyond current levels, remaining at 8 -10 percent of GDP.

⇨ *Official grants* are expected to gradually decline in the next two years from current levels of about 3 percent of GDP to about 1 percent of GDP, as donors reduce assistance.

⇨ *Bilateral and multilateral gross disbursements,* are expected to gradually decline as a result of lower peace-related investment requirements.

⇨ *FDI* prospects will depend on the success of the Government's new development strategy which hinges critically on a marked improvement in the investment climate.

⇨ *Short-term private capital inflows* increased during 1993-94 as a result of wider domestic-international interest rate differentials and peace. Short-term capital inflows may increase in the future as long as: (i) there is a wide interest rate differential; and (ii) El Salvador maintains a consistent, credible market-oriented economic reform program.

The Dutch disease: conceptual framework

The mechanisms through which foreign exchange flows affect the Salvadoran economy are similar to the "Dutch Disease" phenomenon[5] associated with an export boom (in this case remittances or exports of labor) and to the effects of increased capital inflows as experienced by a number of developing countries, particularly in Latin America and East Asia. However, there are two critical differences: (i) *duration* - remittances tend to be more permanent than export booms; and (ii) *uses of foreign exchange receipts* - a much higher portion of remittances tend to be spent on consumption, particularly on non-tradables (NT) relative to imported (or tradable [T]) goods, or re-invested.

These flows have important effects on domestic expenditures, resource allocation and monetary variables. The starting point is an increase in foreign exchange inflows which leads to a higher level of domestic expenditures[6] on both imports and NT goods. The portion spent on imported goods worsens the trade deficit, but has no effect on the money supply or the exchange rate, since it directly accommodates part of the increased supply of foreign exchange. If the whole increase in inflows were spent on imported goods the only concern would be on the sustainability of the financing inflows. The portion spent on NT goods - in a supply-constrained situation - generates a standard macroeconomic transfer problem similar to a Dutch Disease[7] and may lead to:

⇨ **inflationary pressures**: higher demand for NT goods drives up their prices;

⇨ **real exchange rate appreciation** (↓RER): higher NT prices lead to a real exchange rate (RER=Tp/NTp) appreciation, i.e., a rise in the price of NT relative to T goods; the larger the proportion of foreign exchange flows spent on NT goods, the larger the RER appreciation;

⇨ **a decline in the export sector**: the increase in the relative price of NT goods will create incentives to reallocate resources from the export sector to the NT sector and to switch expenditures from NT goods to imports; and

---

[5] See Corden and Neary, 1992; Corden, 1984; van Wijnbergen, 1984; Corbo and Hernández, 1994; and Calvo, Leiderman, and Reinhart, 1993.

[6] Remittances represent an increased transfer from abroad which directly increases income and demand, while capital inflows relax the foreign exchange liquidity constraint.

[7] In the case of El Salvador, these problems are exacerbated by the fact that the marginal propensity to consume NT goods is higher in the case of remittances than for export receipts.

⇨ **short-run monetary disequilibrium:** in an export boom, increased foreign exchange flows (not spent on T goods) result in a balance of payments surplus, an accumulation of international reserves (↑IR), and an expansion of the money supply beyond increases in money demand, generating a <u>short-run</u> excess supply of money. Under a fixed or pre-determined exchange rate regime, NT prices will tend to increase and so would the demand for imports. In the short-run, the monetary expansion will place additional pressure on the RER (↓) but, eventually, the increased demand for imports will solve the disequilibrium. Under flexible exchange rates, the excess supply of money would also put pressure on the nominal exchange rate, generating forces toward a depreciation. However, if the increase in NT prices exceeds the nominal depreciation, in the short-run, the RER will tend to appreciate (Edwards, 1984 and 1986).

Key macroeconomic management issues and the role of the Dutch disease in El Salvador

Inflationary pressures, monetization and domestic credit

High foreign exchange inflows have complicated monetary policy, and in particular, the achievement of the Government's inflation objectives. High foreign exchange flows have contributed to continuing inflationary pressures through two channels: (i) the domestic expenditure effect, i.e., higher NT prices associated with increased consumption driven by remittances; and (ii) monetary disequilibrium, i.e., through the impact of reserve accumulation on monetary expansion. Government efforts at offsetting the inflationary impact of inflows through sterilization policies have been only partially successful. Inflationary pressures persist as a result of the high and inelastic demand for NT goods largely stemming from remittances and from capital inflows to finance public sector expenditures.

Inflation trends. Inflation has been falling but remains well above US and international levels (Figure II.12). The containment of inflationary pressures is critical to the success of the Government strategy since it would enhance competitiveness by limiting the RER appreciation. In addition, lower inflationary expectations will facilitate domestic investment by allowing further expansion of real domestic credit to the private sector.

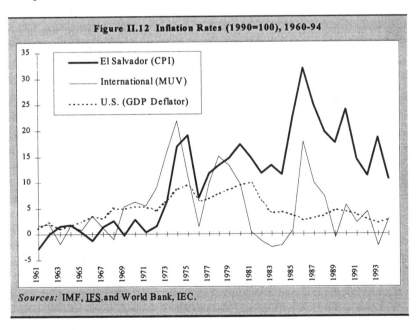

Figure II.12 Inflation Rates (1990=100), 1960-94

— El Salvador (CPI)
— International (MUV)
······ U.S. (GDP Deflator)

Sources: IMF, IFS and World Bank, IEC.

Inflows and monetary disequilibrium. High inflows have exacerbated demand-driven inflationary pressures in El Salvador by raising NT prices and increasing money supply through reserve accumulation. The increase in the money supply (M2)[8] since 1989 reflects the expansion of the monetary base (Figure II.13) associated with high inflows, since net domestic assets have been decreasing during

---

[8] Although mitigating forces included the RER appreciation which has lowered the price of T goods and the financing of the fiscal deficit entirely with foreign resources.

the same period and have been negative since 1993.[9] The pressure of inflows on international reserves has occurred through two reinforcing mechanisms: (i) the portion of foreign exchange spent on NT goods has resulted in a balance of payments surplus (↑IR) and has put pressure on the monetary base; and (ii) Central Bank purchases of foreign exchange to maintain a stable nominal exchange rate led to additional reserve accumulation and further increased the monetary base. Sterilization policies[10] have not been sufficient to completely offset the liquidity-creating effects of inflows because of their high level and the high and inelastic demand for NT goods. In an export boom, the excess money supply is generally only a short-term phenomenon. However, in the case of El Salvador, the impact of inflows on money creation is greater than in an export boom and the automatic adjustment of the monetary sector is much slower, because the marginal propensity to consume NT goods is higher and the demand for NT goods is inelastic owing to the high share of remittances in foreign exchange flows.

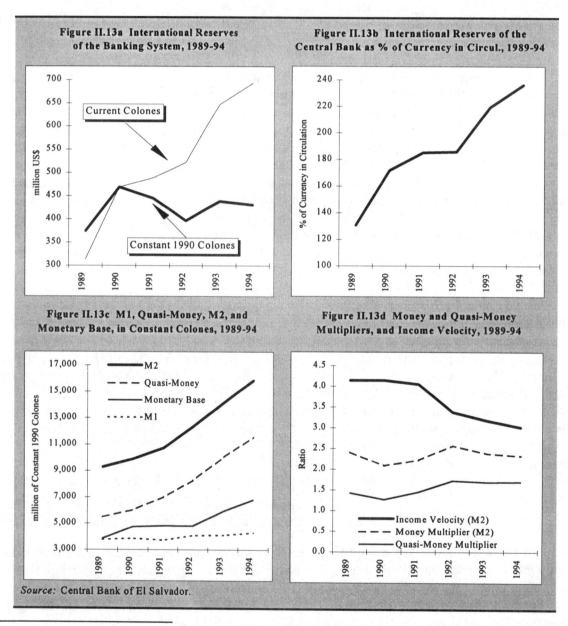

Figure II.13a International Reserves of the Banking System, 1989-94

Figure II.13b International Reserves of the Central Bank as % of Currency in Circul., 1989-94

Figure II.13c M1, Quasi-Money, M2, and Monetary Base, in Constant Colones, 1989-94

Figure II.13d Money and Quasi-Money Multipliers, and Income Velocity, 1989-94

Source: Central Bank of El Salvador.

---

[9]   M2 (money [M1] plus quasi-money [QM]) is used as a proxy for money supply; M2 represents over 90 percent of total banking sector liabilities to the private sector.

[10] Sterilization policies are defined as measures implemented by the Central Bank to offset the impact of the accumulation of international reserves with the objective of containing domestic credit to a level compatible with inflation targets.

Inflows, reserve accumulation, and domestic credit to the private sector. To expand private investment and accelerate growth, inflationary expectations must decline to allow for the necessary increases in credit to the private sector in a non-inflationary manner. The amount of real credit available to the private sector depends on the real cash balances (i.e., money demand, proxied by M2 in real terms) that the public is willing to hold and the amount of net international reserves accumulated by the consolidated banking system. The higher the accumulation of reserves, the lower the availability of real credit.

As a result of increasing inflows, total domestic credit has been contracted to offset the growth in international reserves, contain the increase in money

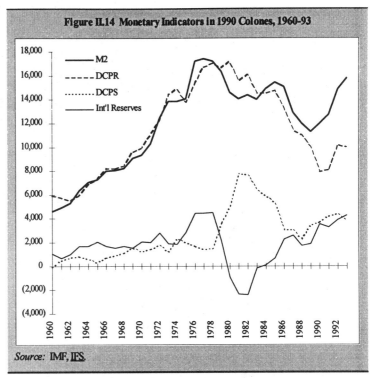

Figure II.14 Monetary Indicators in 1990 Colones, 1960-93

Source: IMF, IFS.

supply and maintain inflation targets. Beginning in 1990, despite continued tight credit policies, an increase in real credit to the private sector was possible thanks to economic growth, increased reliance on foreign financing of the fiscal deficit, and the Government's success in controlling inflation - which was reflected in increasing real cash balances (Figure II.14).

Real exchange rate appreciation

Since the mid-1980s the real exchange rate (RER) has appreciated and exhibited greater variability relative to the previous 25 years. The lower RER is not a problem by itself since it is due to an equilibrium appreciation resulting from an excess supply of dollars associated with higher inflows. However, a certain degree of misalignment is also present, associated with high demand and higher inflation than the main trade partners. The lower RER has contributed to the decline of the export sector, although the decline in real wages has limited the impact of the appreciation on the competitiveness of labor-intensive exports. Given that flows - particularly remittances - are not a temporary phenomenon, policies should aim at ensuring a competitive long-run RER through higher savings (public and private) levels and at avoiding RER misalignment through improved fiscal performance.

Degree of appreciation and variability. A number of bilateral (BRER) and multilateral (MRER) RER indices[11] were computed for 1961-94 (Figure II.15). Three conclusions can be drawn from these indices: (i) the BRER and the MRERs behaved in a similar manner throughout the period,[12] there-

---

[11] The RER measures the relative price of tradable with respect to non tradable goods (RER=Tp/NTp). When the real exchange rate is falling it is appreciating. The bilateral real exchange rate (BRER) is calculated as: BRER = (NER*WPIus)/CPIes, where: NER= the nominal exchange rate; WPIus = the US wholesale price index; CPIes = the Salvadoran consumer price index. The BRER was computed using the dollar because the US is El Salvador's main trade partner. A number of multilateral real exchange rate (MRER) indices were constructed using a basket of currencies. Three groups of countries were used: (i) the top 10 trading partners; (ii) the top 6 non-Latin American trading partners; and (iii) the Central American trading partners. The following weights were used: (i) trade (imports plus exports) [MRERxm]; (ii) exports [MRERx]; and (iii) imports [MRERm]. The weights were calculated for 1978, 1985, and 1991.

[12] The gap between the BRER and the MRERs is larger for the periods in which the US dollar was depreciating relative to other currencies.

fore in the rest of this report the BRER will be used when discussing RER trends; (ii) all indices show a much lower RER for 1980-94 compared to 1961-80;[13] and (iii) since 1985 the RER has remained at a much lower level than in the previous 25 years although with greater variability.

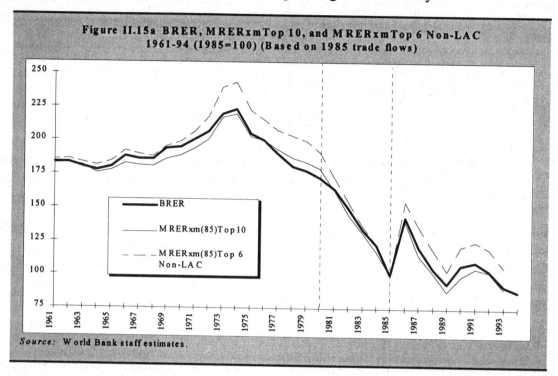

Figure II.15a BRER, MRERxmTop 10, and MRERxmTop 6 Non-LAC 1961-94 (1985=100) (Based on 1985 trade flows)

Source: World Bank staff estimates.

If a wage index is used to calculate the RER - rather than the price index - the BRER exhibits a real depreciation during the last decade. Thus, El Salvador has remained competitive - in labor-intensive exports - relative to its trade competitors. This relative advantage, nevertheless, may be lost if in the future higher real wages are not associated with rapid productivity growth. Finally, it should be stressed that low wages confer comparative advantage only in some goods. In fact, a number of products tend to be exported by high-wage countries, presumably because high wages indicate availability of skilled workers (Leamer and others, 1995).

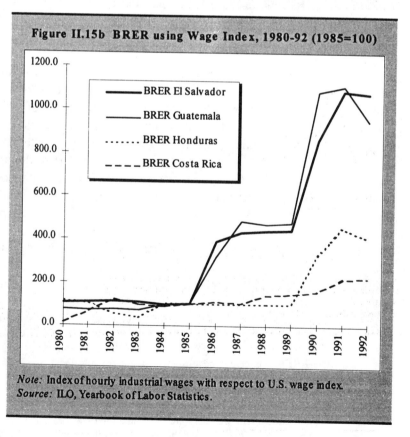

Figure II.15b BRER using Wage Index, 1980-92 (1985=100)

Note: Index of hourly industrial wages with respect to U.S. wage index.
Source: ILO, Yearbook of Labor Statistics.

[13] The two brief RER depreciation episodes after 1985 reflect two large nominal devaluations in 1985 and 1990.

Cross-country comparisons of variability indicators,[14] as calculated by Edwards (1989) show: (i) increasing variability in the 1970s and 1980s, compared to the 1960s; and (ii) an increasing gap between the vola-

Table II.2 Variability Indicators
(MRER - Quarterly Data)

Economy	1965-85		1965-71		1972-85	
	Coefficient of Variation	Difference between Max. and Min.	Coefficient of Variation	Difference between Max. and Min.	Coefficient of Variation	Difference between Max. and Min.
El Salvador	18.10	72.87	3.46	14.19	22.20	72.87
Korea	8.80	42.60	4.87	11.17	6.61	32.70
Thailand	8.14	29.22	3.16	10.10	5.98	25.36
Malaysia	7.59	26.23	3.02	9.70	7.79	26.23
Singapore	6.32	25.15	3.45	10.58	7.23	25.15

Source: Edwards, 1989.

tility of El Salvador's RER compared to high performing East Asian economies (Table II.2). RER variability is important for foreign investors since the higher it is, the higher the risk of operating in the country.

Higher inflows have contributed to the decline of the export sector by lowering the relative price of tradables and leading to resource shifts from the T to the NT sectors. However, relatively lower real wages have benefited the competitiveness of labor-intensive exports. Notwithstanding the strong performance of non-traditional exports, 1994 exports of goods and non factor services as percentage of GDP were less than half their 1974 level (Figure II.17).

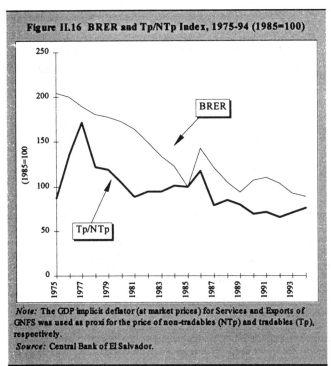

Figure II.16 BRER and Tp/NTp Index, 1975-94 (1985=100)

Note: The GDP implicit deflator (at market prices) for Services and Exports of GNFS was used as proxi for the price of non-tradables (NTp) and tradables (Tp), respectively.
Source: Central Bank of El Salvador.

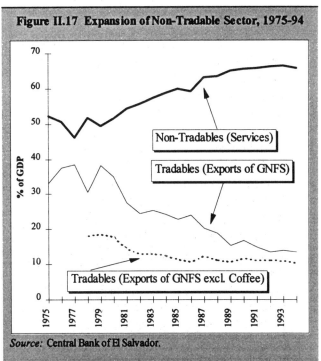

Figure II.17 Expansion of Non-Tradable Sector, 1975-94

Source: Central Bank of El Salvador.

---

[14] Based on calculations of MRERs for 33 countries. The second column shows the difference between the maximum and the minimum values of the indices. These trends are consistent with calculations by Dollar (1992).

RER determinants. RER appreciation reflects structural changes in fundamentals - higher supply of foreign exchange and higher demand for NT goods - which have appreciated the equilibrium RER (ERER) and monetary disequilibria which have contributed to short-run RER misalignment:[15]

⇨ **Role of fundamentals**: high and sustained increases in transfers and capital inflows (Figure II.18) generated forces toward an equilibrium real appreciation through three channels: the direct impact on income; the indirect impact though higher demand for NT goods and higher NT prices; and the indirect impact through short-term monetary disequilibrium. The impact of higher inflows was large enough to compensate for trends in government expenditures, terms of trade, and trade liberalization (Figure II.19) which could have been associated with an equilibrium real depreciation, particularly during 1991-94.

⇨ **Role of monetary variables:** the pursuit of policies to maintain a stable NER since mid-1991 may have also contributed to real appreciation as a result of a Dutch Disease expenditure effect of inflows. In addition, the impact of inflows on monetary expansion through reserve accumulation (1989-94) has reinforced the RER appreciation. As discussed above, in the case of El Salvador this monetary disequilibrium has persisted as a result of the high demand for NT goods.

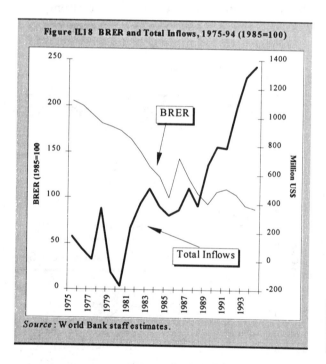

Figure II.18 BRER and Total Inflows, 1975-94 (1985=100)

Source: World Bank staff estimates.

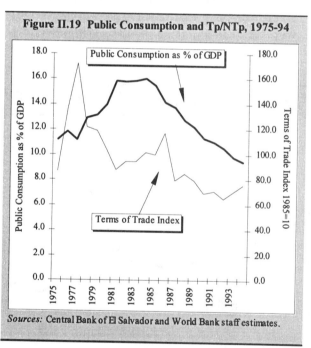

Figure II.19 Public Consumption and Tp/NTp, 1975-94

Sources: Central Bank of El Salvador and World Bank staff estimates.

Exchange rate policy and behavior: historical phases. Figure II.20 suggests that fixed NER periods have been associated with a competitive and stable bilateral RER (BRER) only when inflation has been low and stable. During 1961-74, the BRER slowly depreciated - notwithstanding a fixed NER - as a result of low inflation associated with a very stable macroeconomic environment consistent with the fixed exchange rate regime. During 1975-85, there was a steady RER appreciation to an accumulated 55 percent by 1985; this resulted from: (i) the inflationary impact of the two oil shocks; (ii) the existence of

---

[15] RER misalignment (overvaluation) occurs when the actual RER is below the equilibrium level (RER < ERER), i.e., the actual RER appreciates relative to its long-run equilibrium level; if the RER appreciates in response to an ERER appreciation (resulting from a change in fundamentals) there is no misalignment.

trade and exchange controls, which contributed to the establishment of a parallel foreign exchange market; and (iii) increasing transfers beginning in the late-1970s.[16]

Two characteristics stand out in the 1986-91 period: (i) <u>limited impact of nominal devaluations</u>: the effects of a 100 percent devaluation in January 1986 and a 60 percent devaluation after the unification of the exchange rate (and the establishment of the current flexible exchange rate system) in June 1990 eroded quickly as a result of the increasing supply of dollars. The 1990 devaluation eroded more slowly thanks to trade liberalization, the pre-payment of external debt, and the lifting of restrictions on capital transactions. In 1991 the RER was approximately at the same levels as in 1985; and (ii) <u>significantly lower RER level</u> (more appreciated) compared to the previous two periods.

Since 1989, the authorities have attempted to limit the appreciation of the RER through: (i) policies to lower the excess supply of dollars by accelerating trade liberalization (1989-95) and pre-paying the external debt and oil bills (1991-93); and (ii) policies to contain inflation (1992-95). Since 1991, the Central Bank has pursued sterilized intervention[17] to limit fluctuations of the colón with respect to the US dollar, which has resulted in a very stable NER (a <u>de facto</u> fixed exchange rate). The RER, however, has continued to appreciate during 1994-95 - albeit at a lower rate - as a result of the continued high level of inflows and inflationary pressures.

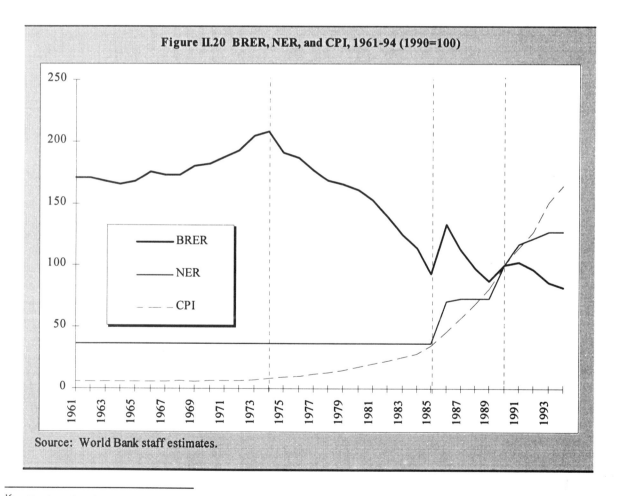

Figure II.20 BRER, NER, and CPI, 1961-94 (1990=100)

Source: World Bank staff estimates.

---

[16] Trade and exchange controls and increasing transfers beginning in the late-1970s also contributed to the appreciation.

[17] In 1990, a flexible exchange-rate system was introduced, but in early 1991, as a result of increasing inflows, the Central Bank began a policy of sterilized intervention, buying foreign exchange to contain the nominal appreciation and in parallel carrying out open-market operations to offset the impact of reserve accumulation on the monetary base.

External viability concerns

There are three key external vulnerability concerns: (i) worsening trade deficits resulting from higher imports associated mostly with remittances coupled with low exports; (ii) current account deficits reflecting high private consumption rather than investment; and (ii) dependence on official grants and short-term flows - rather than medium and long-term flows - to finance current account imbalances. These concerns highlight the need for the Government to support private sector efforts to expand and diversify exports.

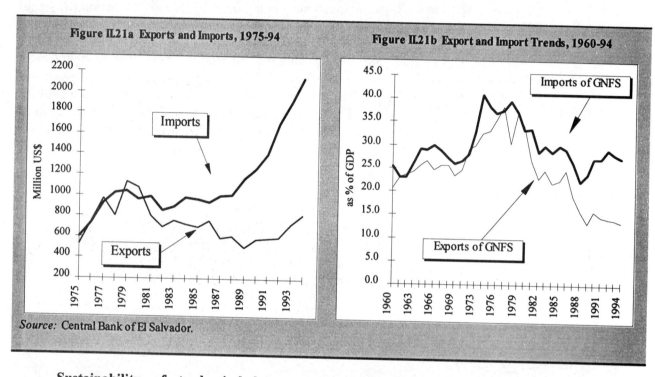

Figure II.21a Exports and Imports, 1975-94

Figure II.21b Export and Import Trends, 1960-94

Source: Central Bank of El Salvador.

Sustainability of trade imbalances. Trade deficits have been increasing mostly as a result of low export growth, rather than high import growth (Figure II.21a and b). **Exports** have been declining since 1978, although this declining trend has been slowly reversing since 1989. The decline in traditional exports (coffee, cotton, sugar, and shrimp) has been partially offset by higher non-traditional exports (Figure II.22), which have significantly expanded and diversified in recent years. By end-1994, however, exports in dollar terms had reached only 1978 levels and as percentage of GDP they were lower than in 1960. Higher inflows, particularly remittances, have also contributed to higher **imports**, through their impact on national income and domestic expenditures. Imports more than doubled in dollar terms since 1988, although as percentage of GDP they remain well below the mid-1970s peak.

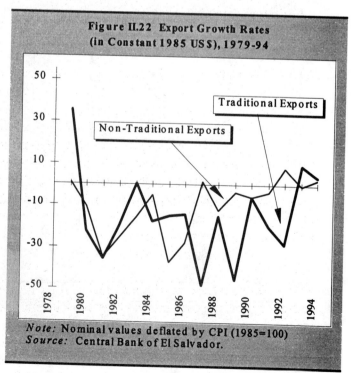

Figure II.22 Export Growth Rates (in Constant 1985 US$), 1979-94

Note: Nominal values deflated by CPI (1985=100)
Source: Central Bank of El Salvador.

Higher imports are currently not a key concern; their levels are still reasonable by historical standards and their impact on the current account has been mitigated by the offsetting impact of remittances (Figure II.23a). It is the performance of the export sector which is particularly worrisome because it also reduces technological progress through *learning by doing* which is largely confined to the traded goods sector, lowers economic growth, and endangers external viability. There is consensus that sustainable current account deficits are, at the most, in the order of 25 percent of exports of goods and services. Currently, El Salvador is below this level but higher export levels are necessary to attain a less vulnerable external position (Figure II.23b).

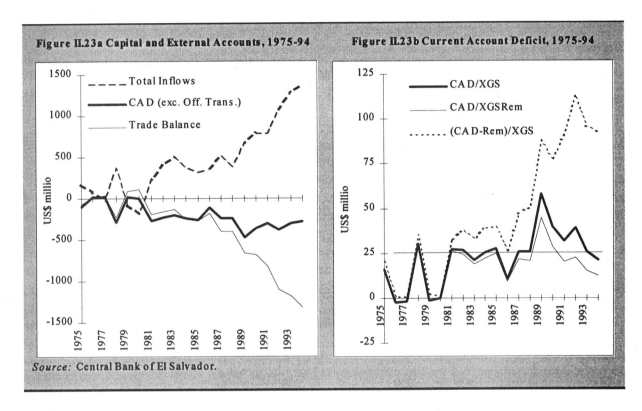

Figure II.23a Capital and External Accounts, 1975-94

Figure II.23b Current Account Deficit, 1975-94

Source: Central Bank of El Salvador.

The main reasons for the slow growth of exports are:

⇨ *worsening terms of trade* and high vulnerability to movements in commodity prices, particularly coffee and cotton. Prospects for improved traditional commodity prices are grim, highlighting the need to further expand and diversify non-traditional exports;

⇨ *structural factors* resulting from remaining constraints to private sector development in general and to exporters in particular; especially, in the areas of infrastructure, technology, production and business services where firms may face difficulties in reaching international technical standards; and, in part,

⇨ *real exchange rate appreciation and resource shifts to the NT sector* resulting from high foreign exchange flows (discussed above).

Low savings and investment. On the expenditure side, current account deficits reflect an excess of expenditure over income; they have been decreasing due to: (i) remittances which have permitted the lowering of the private sector gap despite high private consumption; and (ii) higher public savings. Current account deficits, however, reflect increases in consumption; private consumption is expanding faster than the improvement in public savings. What is of concern is not the increase in consumption - since it has been closely associated with remittances - but the slow growth of investment and private savings (Table II.3).

Table II.3 Savings, Investment, and the Current Account Deficit, 1980-94 (as % of GNP)

	1980-88	1989	1990	1991	1992	1993	1994
Private Investment	8.6	11.5	9.1	10.5	11.3	11.8	12.9
Private Savings	6.9	7.3	4.9	8.9	9.2	10.9	11.5
Private Domestic Savings	5.9	5.9	3.0	6.3	6.3	7.9	8.6
Estimated Savings from Remittances	1.0	1.4	1.9	2.6	2.9	2.9	2.9
Private Sector Gap	1.7	4.2	4.2	1.7	2.1	0.9	1.5
Public Investment	3.9	3.4	2.2	2.4	3.3	3.3	3.2
Public Savings	0.1	-1.5	-0.3	-0.7	0.2	0.6	1.7
Public Sector Gap	3.8	4.9	2.5	3.0	3.1	2.6	1.4
Current Account Gap	5.5	9.2	6.7	4.7	5.2	3.6	2.9
Memo: Investment	12.5	14.9	11.3	12.9	14.6	15.1	16.1
Consumption	92.9	94.2	95.4	91.8	90.6	88.5	86.8
Private Consumption	78.0	82.7	84.5	80.4	79.6	77.8	75.5
Public Consumption	14.9	11.5	10.9	11.4	11.0	10.7	11.4

Source: Central Bank of El Salvador.

Increased dependence on grants and unidentified flows. The basic balance[18] has been increasingly financed through official transfers and errors and omissions. On average, throughout 1975-88, current account deficits were almost completely financed by medium and long term (MLT) capital flows. However, the basic balance became negative beginning in 1983. During 1989-94, while the current account worsened only by about 1.5 percentage points of GDP compared to 1975-88, the basic balance worsened by over 4 percentage points of GDP as a result of lower MLT capital.

This raises the risk of a sudden decrease of current financing flows, i.e., official grants and unidentified sources - possibly short-term private inflows. The current assessment is for external flows to continue at high levels, although their growth rate should be lower. Their composition could continue shifting toward a higher percentage of remittances and possibly larger private flows (foreign investment and short-term flows). As a result, in the medium-term the financing of external deficits should not be an issue, although the balance of payments does remain vulnerable to an unexpected decrease in these flows.

Table II.4 External Deficit and Financing Mechanisms (as % of GDP), 1975-94

	1975-88	1989-94	1989	1990	1991	1992	1993	1994
Current Account Bal. a/	-4.2	-5.7	-9.4	-7.0	-5.0	-5.8	-3.9	-3.2
Trade Balance	-3.7	-14.6	-13.4	-13.3	-13.8	-16.8	-15.5	-15.0
Exports	23.5	9.9	10.0	11.4	9.9	9.1	9.6	9.4
Imports	27.2	24.5	23.4	24.7	23.8	25.9	25.1	24.4
Remittances	2.4	8.8	4.8	6.8	9.2	10.8	10.8	10.7
MLT Capital a/	3.7	1.1	4.1	0.0	-0.9	1.3	1.3	0.5
Basic Balance a/ b/	-0.5	-4.7	-5.3	-7.0	-5.9	-4.4	-2.7	-2.7
Overall Balance	0.3	0.6	-0.7	1.8	-0.9	-0.3	2.0	1.5

a/ Excluding official transfers. b/ Equals Current Account Balance + MLT Capital.
Source: Central Bank of El Salvador.

---

[18] The current account deficit is not necessarily the most appropriate indicator to judge the sustainability of external balances in countries where it is structurally in deficit and has been traditionally financed "autonomously" through long term capital flows. A more appropriate indicator is the basic balance, i.e., the current account adjusted for medium and long term capital flows. This indicator shows that economic growth can be maintained with a current account deficit if it is financed with sufficient medium and long term flows, as occurred in El Salvador, and Central America in general, during the 1960s and 1970s.

Sterilization polices: impact and effectiveness

Since 1991, the authorities have been using sterilization policies to counter the liquidity-creating effects of foreign exchange flows and of their interventions in the foreign exchange market. Concerns have been expressed regarding: (i) the impact of these policies on interest rates and on the Central Bank's operational deficits; and (ii) the effectiveness of these policies. Notwithstanding these concerns, the Salvadoran authorities in the short-term should continue relying on sterilization policies as the main instrument to control monetary expansion because: (i) the level of inflows has stabilized; (ii) the impact on interest rates has not been unduly large, and in any case, the largest component of inflows - remittances - have a low sensitivity to interest rate differentials; and (iii) there is room to improve the operational position of the Central Bank.

The Government announced in mid-1995 its intention to allow a voluntary and gradual dollarization of the economy[19] by eliminating all restrictions on financial operations in US dollars to: (i) enhance the consistency of exchange rate policy with the opening up of the economy and the globalization process; (ii) reducing inflation (by providing a nominal anchor) and interest rates[20] toward US levels; (iii) creating confidence by protecting the domestic currency against speculative attacks and curtailing exchange rate risk; and (iv) enhancing credibility by promoting fiscal and financial discipline.

Instruments of monetary control. The Government's aim of reducing inflation required restraining the growth of bank credit pursued by: (i) decreasing the domestic borrowing requirements of the public sector by increasingly relying on external financing of the fiscal deficit; and (ii) restraining the expansion of credit to the private sector through the use of rediscount, reserve requirements, and open market operations.

During 1992-93 the Central Bank used rediscounts to manage liquidity through the unified rediscount window and the automatic liquidity window. In July 1994 the Central Bank closed its rediscount operations and increased reliance on indirect monetary instruments. Since 1994, the Central Bank has relied exclusively on reserve requirements and open-market operations. After several increases between 1989 (19 percent for local currency deposits) and 1993 (between 20 and 30 percent), reserve requirements on bank liabilities in local currency have remained unchanged. However, in July 1994 the Central Bank established temporary investment requirements in the form of holdings of Stabilization Certificates (CEMs - *Certificados de Estabilización Monetaria*). In addition, to further tighten credit policy, the Superintendency of the Financial System (SSF) increased provisioning requirements on certain loans. The Central Bank initiated open-market operations - with CEMs - in July 1991. CEMs have shown: (i) decreasing volume, particularly since late-1994 (Figures II.24a and b); (ii) continued prevalence of Bank and non-bank financial institutions as major holders; and (iii) increasing share of longer term (360 days) bonds.

Impact on interest rates. The need to issue CEMs has put upward pressure on interest rates. Although in relation to dollar rates, domestic interest rates are significantly higher, in view of the relatively low level of real interest rates on deposits, and considering that bank interest rate spreads are in the range of 5 - 10 percentage points, the real cost of borrowing might not be characterized as high, after incorporating credit and market risk factors.

---

[19] Originally, the Government had announced on February 3, 1995 its intention of moving to a currency board-type system, sanctioning the return to a fixed exchange rate regime as a transition measure prior to the move to full dollarization.

[20] Reflecting the fall in devaluation expectations.

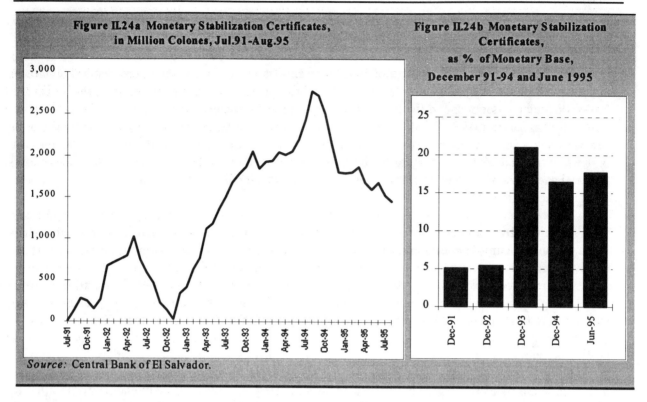

Figure II.24a Monetary Stabilization Certificates, in Million Colones, Jul.91-Aug.95

Figure II.24b Monetary Stabilization Certificates, as % of Monetary Base, December 91-94 and June 1995

Source: Central Bank of El Salvador.

At least since mid-1993, interest rates on commercial bank deposits have remained consistently above the equivalent rate on CEMs. It appears that active intervention by the Central Bank has led to a market-determined premium on deposit rates over the CEM rate as financial intermediaries have used the CEM rates as a floor for their own deposit rates.

The interest rate on 180 day deposits has been consistently above the implied rate on US dollar deposits based on the US Fed Funds rate. This yield differential could induce the following market responses: (i) domestic investors will have a preference for domestic interest-bearing deposits; and (ii) domestic investors may repatriate some of the capital invested abroad in order to benefit from the higher domestic interest rate. However, the latter source of capital inflows should be regarded as volatile deposits, which could swiftly be taken out of the country if domestic/foreign interest rates fall/rise, or if a currency devaluation is anticipated. Remittances are not sensitive to interest rate differentials since

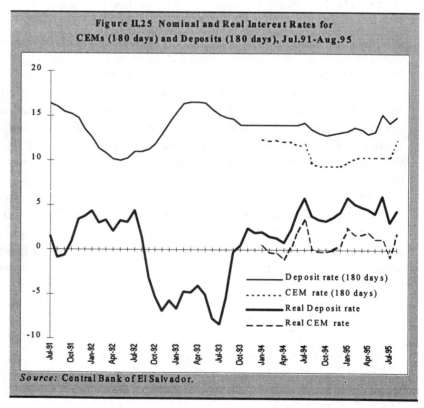

Figure II.25 Nominal and Real Interest Rates for CEMs (180 days) and Deposits (180 days), Jul.91-Aug.95

Deposit rate (180 days)
CEM rate (180 days)
Real Deposit rate
Real CEM rate

Source: Central Bank of El Salvador.

most of these transfers are used to support the consumption needs of the beneficiaries.

Impact on Central Bank operational losses. The costs of sterilization have contributed to the operational losses of the Central Bank[21] through : (i) the interest differential between higher holdings of low-yield foreign assets and the costs of servicing high-yield domestic bonds; and (ii) the debt service cost of CEMs. During 1994-95, interest on CEMs is expected to be the second largest component of the Central Bank's interest expense, after interest on reserve requirements. During 1990-92, Central Bank deficits represented about 0.9 percent of GDP. In 1993, losses fell to about 0.2 percent due mostly to the renewed payments of interest obligations by the Central Government.

There is still room to further lower Central Bank operational losses, through actions to: (i) ensure timely payment by the Government of market determined interest rates on its liabilities to the Central Bank (already incorporated in the proposed Central Bank Reform Law); (ii) promote issuance of the Government's own paper to cover short-term financing needs. This will be introduced under the Central Bank Reform Law, although the issuance of Government instruments should include both Treasury Notes (short-term) and Bonds (long-term); and (iii) establish a reserve account to cover interest arrears and non-recoverable assets from the operations of FOSAFFI.[22] This reserve should be funded by the Government directly, or through a special assessment on the commercial banks to be derived from net profits.

Effectiveness and sustainability. The key variables in analyzing the effectiveness of sterilization operations and the appropriate response to large inflows are: (i) the exchange rate regime; (i) the degree of financial liberalization and development; (ii) the source of the disturbance; and (iii) the duration of the inflows (Frankel, 1994). The conventional view is that sterilization policies are ineffective under fixed exchange rates and perfect capital mobility (i.e., there is no scope for an independent monetary policy as measured by both interest rates and the money supply). The assumption being that the domestic interest rate is tied to the exogenous foreign interest rate and potentially infinite rates of capital flows will respond to changes in domestic interest rates. Sterilization under a fixed exchange rate regime can be effective, but only in the short-run. In the longer-run, sterilization tends to exacerbate capital inflows because of the differential between domestic and foreign interest rates (Calvo, 1991; and Calvo, Leiderman, and Reinhart, 1993).

El Salvador is currently characterized by: (i) a flexible nominal exchange rate which, however, has been maintained at a stable rate of approximately 8.75 colones per dollar since 1993 through Central Bank intervention; (ii) high level of remittances which are largely insensitive to interest rate differentials; (iii) the source of the disturbance - high inflows, mostly remittances - is similar to an export boom; and (iv) continuing high inflows but more stable. Under these conditions, interest rates will indeed be higher than they would have been in absence of the flows but sterilization polices should continue to be effective in limiting monetary expansion given the low sensitivity of remittances to interest rate differentials. Eventually, the more integrated El Salvador becomes with the world capital market, the more elastic the supply of funds will become and relatively high real domestic interest rates would trigger interest-sensitive flows.

---

[21] Additional causes include: (i) sizable holdings of low interest Government debt which is frequently in arrears; and (ii) costs incurred during the restructuring and privatization of banks and finance companies. The interest cost of the bonds fluctuates with market interest rates, and represented the largest component of interest expense in 1993.

[22] The *Fondo de Saneamiento y Fortalecimiento Financiero*, the entity which carried out the restructuring and recapitalization of the commercial banks and finance companies prior to privatization.

Recommendations: macroeconomic management with high foreign exchange flows

Policy constraints. The analysis in this Chapter highlights the following considerations and constraints in the development of the remaining macroeconomic agenda:

⇨   **Implications and requirements of peace.** As has been the case in other countries in the aftermath of a prolonged civil war there has been little peace dividend in the short-run (World Bank 1994). This is mostly because private investment and government revenue are slow to recover and there is a pending need to repair damaged infrastructure. In addition, at least in the short-run, the consolidation of peace requires additional outlays to not only finance peace-related expenditures (particularly the reintegration of ex-combatants into economic life) but also to alleviate poverty and address the social roots of the civil war.

⇨   **Sustained high foreign exchange flows and equilibrium RER appreciation.** There is a consensus in the literature that the sustainability of capital inflows is the critical parameter for policy design. The higher level of foreign exchange flows entails a change in the underlying structure of the economy, and in particular the equilibrium appreciation of the RER. Moreover, as the country develops, increases productivity, maintains high growth rates, and continues to attract capital, a gradual appreciation of the RER is to be expected.

⇨   **The impact of high and sustained increase in demand for NT goods,** as a result of remittances and the fact they are mostly used to buy non-tradable goods. This exacerbates the monetary implications of inflows and worsens the RER appreciation.

⇨   **Implications of the Government's commitment to maintaining the stability of the nominal exchange rate.** This position constrains the use of the exchange rate as an instrument of macroeconomic policy and highlights the critical importance of fiscal policy.

Policy recommendations. In the short-term, the Government should continue open market operations to sterilize excess inflows. However, sterilization polices impose costs in the financial system and in the longer-term more fundamental cures must be implemented to adjust to the higher level of foreign exchange flows. These policies would not only be beneficial <u>per se</u>, but would also have a buffer effect in the event of further increases in private capital inflows resulting from on-going economic reforms. The authorities should therefore focus on:

⇨   First, and foremost, **strengthen fiscal performance**, while ensuring enough fiscal space to finance peace-related and social expenditures. The macro policy balance should favor relatively tighter fiscal rather than monetary policy. The credibility of exchange rate and monetary policy does not depend on fixing the exchange rate, but pursuing consistent and credible macroeconomic policies. A stronger fiscal performance is key to: (i) ensure moderate inflation and the credibility of exchange rate and monetary policy; i.e., a fiscal anchor is the only way to enhance credibility and lower inflationary expectations; (ii) lower the level of inflows by decreasing external financing requirements; (iii) ensure non-inflationary increases in domestic credit to the private sector, which will be possible only if domestic financing requirements of the public sector continue to decline and inflationary expectations decrease; and (iv) counter the effect on interest rates by both the growth in private demand and any required open market operations to reduce excess liquidity.

The experience of successful East Asian economies (Corbo and Hernández, 1994; and Wang and Shilling, 1995) shows that a mix of fiscal-monetary policy seems to be more appropriate in the short-run since fiscal policy usually lacks the required flexibility to deal quickly with volatile capital flows. However, sterilized intervention is also most effective when accompanied by fiscal restraint. Tight fiscal policy seems to be the best way to maximize benefits from capital inflows while reducing their side effects, especially real exchange rate appreciation. In the long-run, increased public savings appear to be the only way to protect the real exchange rate. This is also the type of policy perceived more favorably by international investors.

⇨ **Raise national savings.** Higher savings are critical to reduce absorption and improve management of inflows in the long-run. Results from a recent international comparative analysis of savings behavior (Edwards 1995) suggest a number of possible policy measures to begin raising savings, including: (i) increasing the depth and efficiency of the financial sector; (ii) reforming the social security system; and (iii) increasing public savings, since higher public savings appear not to be fully offset by declines in private savings, thus increasing overall savings rates.

⇨ **Relieve inflationary pressures** fueled by the high proportion of inflows spent on NT goods by: (i) encouraging higher domestic savings; (ii) lowering government consumption, which is usually biased toward NT goods; (iii) fostering private investment, which is usually more T good-intensive; and (iv) in the longer-term, ensuring that a larger percentage of private inflows are in the form of foreign direct investment.

⇨ **Pursue a credible exchange rate policy.** The colón has experienced an equilibrium real appreciation. The continuation of high inflows and economic growth entail a change in the underlying structure of the economy, and in particular, a lower RER. To avoid short-run RER misalignment, the authorities should continue to focus on ensuring consistent macroeconomic polices and moderating inflation. Moreover, there are a number of policy actions the Government can focus on to generate a long-run RER depreciation: (i) accelerate trade liberalization (to increase demand for T goods); (ii) lower foreign exchange flows by improving fiscal performance and decreasing the external financing needs of the public sector; and (iii) increase national savings. If the economy does voluntarily dollarize, the Government should accelerate on-going policies to: (i) improve fiscal performance; (ii) strengthen the efficiency and depth of the financial system through improved prudential supervision, deposit insurance, and capital markets development; and (iii) ensure continued labor market flexibility.

⇨ **Facilitate expansion and diversification of exports**. External sector vulnerability and sustainability concerns highlight the need to increase the level of exports. Moreover, given price and demand expectations for traditional commodities, efforts should be geared at shifting resources so as to further diversify products and markets. A distortion-correction approach to export promotion is the most consistent with optimal trade policy theory, policy experience, and political economy considerations. As a result of the equilibrium appreciation of the RER the scope for increasing export profitability though a higher RER is limited The Government should continue supporting private sector efforts to increase productivity and improve global competitiveness within a context of a lower RER, by: (i) assuring a stable macroeconomic environment; (ii) removing general constraints to private investment through the implementation of reforms to improve labor and infrastructure (Chapter III); modernize the legal and regulatory environment (Chapter IV) and strengthen the financial sector (Chapter VI); and (iii) removing specific constraints to export growth (Chapter V).

CHAPTER III

IMPROVING LABOR AND INFRASTRUC

An educated and skilled labor force, coupled with efficient and flexible lat conditions for the success of the Government's development strategy. In a dollariz market flexibility is even more critical to respond to external shocks and to contain in vador the labor market appears to be relatively competitive, but the lack of skilled work ...ow labor productivity may be the key bottleneck to accelerating growth. This chapter reviews labor market characteristics and trends, and discusses constraints and policy options to: ensure the availability of skilled labor and enhance its productivity; lower labor costs; and improve contractual flexibility and labor management relations.

El Salvador cannot fulfill its potential for export-led growth without overhauling its infrastructure. Its poor condition saps the competitiveness of the private sector, as efficient services are increasingly important to firms' capacity to compete in world markets. This chapter also provides: an overview of infrastructure; approaches to the provision of infrastructure services; and suggested guidelines for managing change including a summary of issues and opportunities in key sectors.

DEVELOPING HUMAN RESOURCES AND LABOR MARKETS

Labor market characteristics and trends

Characteristics. Despite high migration, El Salvador has **high labor force growth rates**, in the order of 3 percent per year since 1980, compared to East Asia (between 2 and 2.6 percent) and Latin American (2.4 percent) during the same period. However, the labor force remains **largely unskilled** (Figure III.1). It is notable that while the mean years of education for the Salvadoran labor force is around 4.4, it is 8.7 for Salvadoran immigrants to the US (Montes, 1987). Labor force participation is high and rising (55 percent urban and 37 percent female).

Urban Labor Market Trends, 1988-93. The urban labor market shows: (i) **increasing labor force participation** (Figure III.2) to some extent due to the end of the civil war, resulting in the absorption of ex-combatants and increased economic activity; and (ii) **increasing employment** and lower open unemployment rates

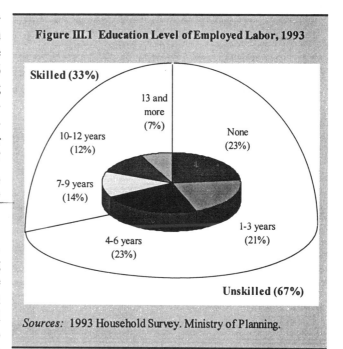

Figure III.1 Education Level of Employed Labor, 1993

Skilled (33%)

13 and more (7%)

None (23%)

10-12 years (12%)

7-9 years (14%)

1-3 years (21%)

4-6 years (23%)

Unskilled (67%)

Sources: 1993 Household Survey. Ministry of Planning.

(Figure III.3). The informal sector has became an important source of additional employment opportunities. El Salvador has a **relatively flexible urban labor market**, at least by Latin American standards. Labor turnover rates (over 10 percent) and the relationships between real wages, employment and GDP growth are fairly consistent with a flexible and competitive labor market (Figure III.4), which holds for

...d formal employment. Sectoral shifts in employment and individual periods of unemployment ...also consistent with flexible labor markets.[1]

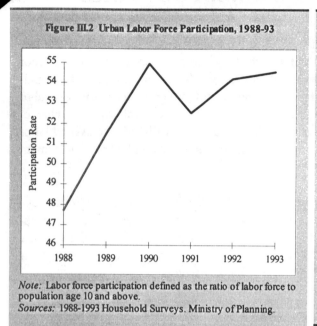

Figure III.2 Urban Labor Force Participation, 1988-93

Note: Labor force participation defined as the ratio of labor force to population age 10 and above.
Sources: 1988-1993 Household Surveys. Ministry of Planning.

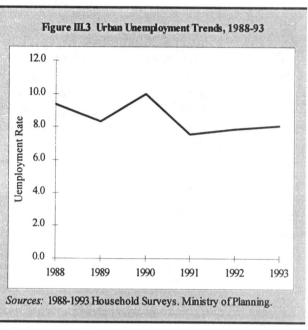

Figure III.3 Urban Unemployment Trends, 1988-93

Sources: 1988-1993 Household Surveys. Ministry of Planning.

Recently, there has been **a halt in the sharp decline in real wages** observed during the 1980s. Falling real wages indicate that labor market adjustments have been achieved largely through changes in real wages. Private consumption per capita, however, has remained approximately constant due to remittances. Finally, there is a **modest gap between skilled and unskilled wages**, which appears to indicate a non-segmented market (Figures III.5a, b, and c).

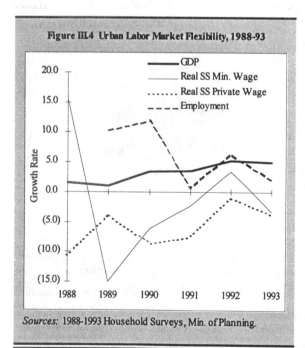

Figure III.4 Urban Labor Market Flexibility, 1988-93

GDP — Real SS Min. Wage — Real SS Private Wage — Employment

Sources: 1988-1993 Household Surveys, Min. of Planning.

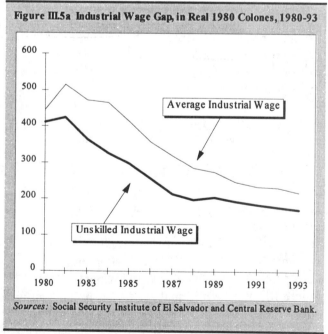

Figure III.5a Industrial Wage Gap, in Real 1980 Colones, 1980-93

Average Industrial Wage

Unskilled Industrial Wage

Sources: Social Security Institute of El Salvador and Central Reserve Bank.

---

[1] The most flexible sectors appear to be agriculture and services. The last job of the unemployed in the whole labor force is 43 percent in agriculture, 13 percent in services, and 10 percent in industry; and, for urban workers, 20 percent in services, 13.5 percent in agriculture and 13 percent in industry. Individual periods of unemployment are relatively short, less than three months on average. Only 20 percent of the unemployed have individual unemployment periods of over a year.

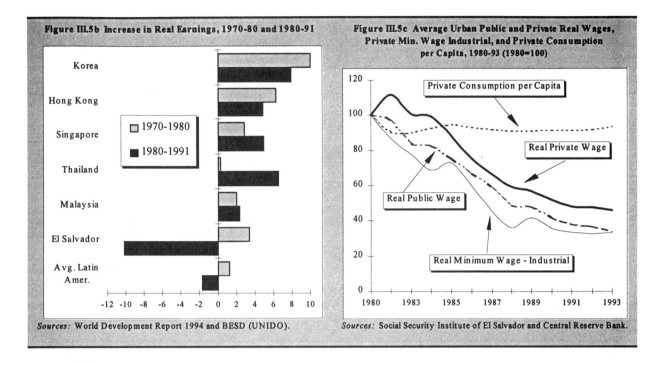

Figure III.5b Increase in Real Earnings, 1970-80 and 1980-91

Figure III.5c Average Urban Public and Private Real Wages, Private Min. Wage Industrial, and Private Consumption per Capita, 1980-93 (1980=100)

Sources: World Development Report 1994 and BESD (UNIDO).

Sources: Social Security Institute of El Salvador and Central Reserve Bank.

Developing human resources and enhancing productivity

The lack of skilled workers and low productivity is the key bottleneck to accelerating growth and the leading problem in labor markets. The seriousness of this constraint was confirmed by the survey results, where the most important labor constraint was the availability of skilled workers. What is even more worrisome, the human resource constraint came in first place when entrepreneurs were asked an open ended question (a general question, with no multiple choice answers) on constraints to firms. The potential for productivity growth is hampered by: (i) education and health sector weaknesses and a surplus of largely unskilled labor; and (ii) the limited absorptive capacity of high-return sectors and firms' limited ability to adopt new technologies. A comprehensive review of the education and health sectors is contained in two recent World Bank reports - The Challenge of Poverty Alleviation (June 1994) and Decentralization and Community Education Strategy (December 1994) - and in the background documentation of two projects currently under preparation - a Basic Education Project and a Health Reform Project. To address this bottleneck, the authorities should continue ongoing efforts to:

✓ ensure a growing supply of skilled labor through education sector reforms;
✓ support private sector efforts to develop an active and comprehensive training policy; and
✓ contribute to the quality and efficiency of the labor supply through health sector reforms.

Lowering direct and indirect labor costs

Decreasing and simplifying direct labor costs. Constraints include stratified minimum wages, excessive overtime premia and lack of productivity compensation. First, minimum wages are set by sector, economic activity, and crop (in agriculture). There is little economic justification for such a practice since there is little evidence of monopsony power or lack of mobility. Second, the wage differential between the formal and the informal sectors suggests that the opportunity cost of leisure is low and thus that the hardship compensation for overtime (100 percent) and night shifts (25 percent) is excessive. The premia unreasonably raise economic costs and can have adverse substitution and scale effects. Third, while there are no legal obstacles to productivity-linked compensation schemes, they are generally absent in the private sector.

To decrease and simplify direct labor costs the Government could: (i) unify minimum wages; (ii) set the minimum wage unit as the hourly rate, rather than the daily rate, to facilitate measurement, usage and accounting; and (iii) introduce productivity-linked compensation. There has been an apparent, albeit imperfect, attempt at indexing the minimum wage since 1990, which should be discouraged. It has affected employment in the formal sector and in parts of agriculture. The emphasis should be on linking compensation with productivity gains. Higher real wages should follow.

Decreasing non-wage labor costs. Non-wage labor costs are significant, particularly given the low quality of services provided from the proceeds of employment taxes. However, these costs are below the regional average. These non-wage costs are distortionary as they are assessed against the wage bill and encourage inefficient substitution between labor and capital. They can also have undesirable scale effects. The generally weak link between payments and expected benefits compounds the distortion. To decrease non-wage labor costs, overtime and night shift wage premia should be cut significantly. Premia of 50 percent for overtime and 15 percent for night shifts are common elsewhere.

Eliminating the negative impact of public sector wages and employment policies. The most severe employment and wage distortions appear in the public sector, including: (i) human resource management weaknesses; (ii) full job security granted to civil servants by the Civil Service Law; (iii) wage distortions created by the remuneration policy for public servants; (iv) shorter working hours than in the private sector (a 7.3-hour working day compared with 8 hours in the private sector); (v) overstaffing; (vi) lack of competitive procedures in recruitment; and (vii) lack of an incentive-based compensation system. The impact of these public sector wage and employment distortions on private sector development is multiple: the remuneration of public employees affects the level of wages paid by the private sector; the extent of overemployment and its cost has an impact on the fiscal burden borne by the private sector; and the quality and efficiency of public services affects the costs and productivity of private sector operations.

To address the negative impact of public sector wages and employment policies the Government should accelerate implementation of the on-going civil service reform, and in particular: (i) strengthen human resource management; (ii) revise the Civil Service Law so as to eliminate job security and bring daily working hours in line with the private sector; (iii) reduce overstaffing through incentives and voluntary retirement programs; (iv) revise salary scales and introduce performance-linked compensation schemes, particularly in state enterprises; and (v) implement competitive and objective procedures for the selection, evaluation and promotion of public employees.

Contracting flexibility and labor management relations

Maintaining contracting flexibility. There are no major obstacles, legal or otherwise, to contracting or shedding labor and the cost-severance payments are relatively low by Latin American standards. This conclusion was confirmed by the survey. Obstacles related to contracting inflexibility, labor management relations, labor regulations, and union activity were ranked the lowest among Latin American countries surveyed to date. Some 14 percent of enterprises had unionized workers, concentrated primarily among construction firms and roughly correlated with size. However, only 6 percent had experienced a strike in the last five years. Firing appears to be easy, and some 64 percent of enterprises reported having dismissed a worker in the last year for any reason. The process averaged about three days, depending on the enterprise's own policies.

Labor turnover rates, while slightly lower than international standards, are reasonable and do not appear to show locking-in of employment. Furthermore, the data are for 1992-93, a period of significant growth of the kind usually characterized by lower than average turnover rates. As might have been expected, turnover rates are higher for small firms (10.5 percent) than for larger ones (? the result of the lower separation costs - direct and indirect - of small firms. Indirec arise from sunk training costs and potential labor strife costs, particularly in unioniz are higher for larger firms. The sectors with the highest turnover rates, agricul those with the highest contracting flexibility, little training and minimal unioniz voluntary training costs could be the major constraint to labor adjustment, since labor force makes it difficult and costly to replace trained workers.

Improving dispute resolution procedures. Effective procedures to resolve labor-management conflicts are even more important with the approval of reforms to the Labor Code (April 21, 1994) which will likely produce an increase in unionization. An increase in conflicts and disputes is therefore likely, which adds to the importance of effective conflict resolution procedures that diminish the likelihood and duration of strikes. Key areas are the limited use of oral procedures and the lack of compulsory mediation.

Oral procedures are used only when disputes are below 200 colones (about US$23). Otherwise, written proceedings are used, which are more costly and time consuming, and place and added burden on the court system. Moreover, the reformed Labor Code provides for mediation if demanded by one of the parties. Compulsory arbitration is possible only if demanded by both parties (except for essential services). Furthermore, arbitration and mediation are used only in collective conflict cases, not in individual conflict, which is unwarranted. In 1991 2,069 individual conflicts were registered compared with 26 collective conflict cases. More than half the individual cases ended up in court, thus clogging up the court system, increasing costs and causing unnecessary delays. To improve dispute resolution procedures the Government could: (i) expand the use of oral proceedings, allowing for exceptions; (ii) establish a requirement for compulsory arbitration, beyond the essential services clause, with a legal right of appeal; and (iii) extend compulsory mediation and arbitration to individual conflict cases.

MODERNIZING INFRASTRUCTURE

Overview

Mounting problem. El Salvador entered the 1990s with under-developed and under-maintained infrastructure, poorly adapted to the demands of a dynamic, export-led market economy. Telecommunications, power, transport, water and waste services deteriorated during the civil war. Security expenditures crowded out spending on basic maintenance and investment, and acts of war heavily damaged the power and transport networks. The wartime economy was also marked by strong state intervention in the pricing and delivery of services. Energy, telecommunications and water were merged into vertically-integrated, state-owned monopolies. Regulatory and executive functions were not clearly separated, and worse, the companies performed both but were not responsible for either. Rate-setting, investment decisions, procurement, financial oversight, and other key responsibilities were diffused across many institutions. Large numbers of surplus employees were hired. Competition in service provision was minimal, with little private participation. Prices were not adjusted for two decades, and then only for inflation or devaluation. With the exception of the lucrative telecommunications monopoly, the utility companies became dependent on ever larger government bail-outs. By the war's end, the Government was saddled with a daunting backlog of maintenance and investment, which translated into large unmet demand and frequent interruptions of service (Table III.1).

Table III.1 Telecommunications, Road and Power Infrastructure in the region, 1992

	Telephone main lines		Paved roads		Electricity generation capacity		Electricity production	
	connections	per 100 pop.	km	per 1000 pop.	kw	per 100 pop.	kwH (m)	kwH per 100 pop.
Central America								
Costa Rica	364,100	11.8	5,600	2.00	1,009,000	33	4,109	132,600
El Salvador	204,000	3.9	1,936	0.37	697,900	13	2,382	44,970
Guatemala	231,100	2.3	3,485	0.38	769,000	8	2,822	28,090
Honduras	117,100	2.2	2,400	0.47	540,500	10	2,315	44,090
Nicaragua	66,800	2.1			427,000	13	1,616	49,840
Panama	265,500	11.1	2,360	0.98	956,200	40	3,030	126,220
Mexico	6,753,700	7.5	82,022	0.95	29,274,000	34	122,482	142,090

Notes: Paved roads figures are from 1992 for El Salvador, and 1990 for all other countries.
Electricity generation and production figures are from 1990 for the U.S. and Mexico.
Source: World Development Report 1994, ANTEL, CEL, Ministerio Obras Publicas El Salvador.

The view from the private sector. Deficiencies in the quality and quantity of infrastructure continue to hamper private sector growth, according to the survey, particularly the relative severity of telecommunications, highway and power problems. Not only did they top the list of infrastructure-related concerns for the sample as a whole, but they were the uppermost infrastructure concerns of important groups of firms: industrial and commerce, large and medium-sized, export-oriented and non-exporting, and those in San Salvador where one quarter of the country's population resides. Exporting firms are bothered most by the poor condition of the highways. Moreover, developers of Free Trade Zones reported serious delays in obtaining sites, telephone, power and water services.

Infrastructure provision: approaches and lessons of experience

The Government recognizes that poor performance of state-owned enterprises is largely responsible for infrastructure bottlenecks, lagging investment and unmet demand, and the lack of access of the poor; that technological change and advances in applied economics have stripped some infrastructure monopolies of their "naturalness," lowering barriers to entry and subjecting sectors to competition, if not in the market, then for the market; and that good economic regulation of natural monopolies can promote economic welfare and afford investors and consumers sufficient protection against potential abuses. The Government also recognizes practical constraints. The scale of investment required to satisfy pent-up demand, let alone support an export-led growth strategy, is far beyond its financial capacity. Significant private investment, foreign and domestic, will have to be mobilized to close the infrastructure gap. The success of the export-led growth strategy will hinge partly on closing this gap. Surveys of multinationals often cite infrastructure quality as one of the most critical factors in influencing decisions on the location of investments in manufacturing and high-technology sectors.

As the Government reassesses its role in each infrastructure sector, it is useful to frame the analysis with four broad considerations:

⇨ whether a service is publicly or privately owned and managed, it should be run on a commercial basis with prices covering costs, and any subsidies, provided directly and transparently;
⇨ creating a market structure that maximizes opportunities for competition is critical;
⇨ as non-competitive elements are unbundled from competitive or potentially-competitive ones, as a rule, the former will require continuing oversight or regulation to protect investors and consumers from abuses. While the form of regulation will depend on a country's institutional endowment, it should ideally be organized at arm's length from the Government, and operate under rules that are clear, expeditious, credible, and stable; and

⇨ a growing body of research and recent Latin American experience suggest that private ownership and management are most effective in locking in gains from commercialization and competition.

Seizing opportunities: general recommendations

The legacy of the 1980s has been highly negative for infrastructure. The Government must overcome the huge backlog of maintenance and investment in order to improve the quantity and quality of infrastructure while, at the same time, transforming the role of the state and inviting the private sector to become a new partner in these activities. This change in the relationship between the state and the private sector is, indeed, the only way to address the needs for increased management skills and finance. The foundation for this transformation has been established and some steps, e.g., in power, have been taken. The agenda of policy and institutional change in each infrastructure sector involves:

✓ **revising the basic legal framework of governance**, to separate the policy-making and regulatory functions of government (national, subnational, or municipal) from the operational functions, and clearly define responsibilities for all public and private entities involved in the sector;

✓ **reforming market structures within sectors** (breaking down the vertically integrated entities), to unbundle truly natural monopoly components from competitive or potentially competitive activities-thereby permitting competition both *in* and *for* market segments;

✓ **articulating in detail the new government role in regulation**, which involves: (i) for natural monopolies defining regulatory policies to protect investors and the public interest, stipulated in statutes or contracts between public and private entities; and (ii) creating institutional mechanisms and implementation capacity to carry out this regulatory function. A key will be to ensure *a politically independent approach for tariff policy* based on sound economic and financial criteria;

✓ **specifying the financial role of government**: (i) the subsidy policy, if any, that is justified to compensate operators for non-remunerative but essential services; any subsidies transferred directly to target groups need to be identified and financed; (ii) in activities where the State will retain a significant role, (e.g., non-toll roads) a secure institutional framework is needed to ensure financing of maintenance and accountability to users (e.g., a road board funded by road user charges);

✓ **promoting private sector participation** in the reformed system, which may require proactive support for at least a transitional period. At a minimum, there is a need to create a transparent, streamlined process of contract design, competitive bidding, and screening/approval of transactions; ensuring that new entrants compete fairly with incumbent operators; and removing constraints to competition, such as limited access to market information.

✓ **in those activities which remain**, transitionally or for the longer term, **under public ownership and operation** - such as (in most countries) the transmission of power and the main road network - **restructuring of the responsible entity is needed** to create incentives for efficient, commercial operation and to permit even limited private sector involvement, such as through contracting-out services or management. This restructuring may require corporatization, downsizing, decentraliza-tion, and improvement of financial and management information systems.

These six broad categories of policy and institutional reforms are not a chronological sequence, although most countries begin with the first and the last; each step is mutually reinforcing and needs to progress in concert. However, the full agenda is enormously demanding to countries with limited institutional capacity and each country has to find its own pace and sequence. Moreover, there is a range of choices regarding strategies and organizations to meet reform objectives. International experience suggests two clear lessons, with special significance for countries with limited institutional capacity such as El Salvador: (i) choices which allow greater scope for competition provide stronger incentives for good performance, while reducing regulatory requirements; and (ii) allowing extensive private participation (in management, financing, and ownership) - in ways that permit it to absorb risks as well as the rewards of good performance - improve the prospects for successful outcomes.

Telecommunications

Structure. Since 1963, the state-owned company, *Administración Nacional de Telecomunicaciones* (ANTEL), has been the sole provider of basic telephone service, with the power to license or grant concessions for value-added services. In recent years, ANTEL has allowed private operators to offer value-added services, although competition remains weak. A cellular operator was granted a five-year concession and by 1994 had 1,500 subscribers. Its charges are high by international standards: firms paid US$1,000 for a connection and 35 cents a minute in 1993, compared, for example, with only US$100 and 16 cents a minute in Sri Lanka, where there are four licensed operators. Data transmission facilities have been leased to a private operator, with three to four more leases to be negotiated soon. A paging service has also been licensed.

Performance. El Salvador's telecommunications sector has been among the weakest in Latin America. In 1989 there were just 2.9 lines per 100 inhabitants, which compared favorably only with the poorer neighboring countries of Nicaragua (1.2), Honduras (1.9) and Guatemala (2.2). Network expansion, though, lagged even these neighbors. In 1981-91, the network grew 5.9 percent annually compared with 11.4 percent in Honduras and 7.5 percent in Guatemala. As a result, El Salvador had by 1992 the longest waiting list for telephone lines in Central America. Many of the sector's weaknesses are due to the inefficiency of ANTEL. In 1989, it operated with fewer lines per employee (22) than all Central American carriers, except Nicaragua (16). Unrelated activities have yet to be contracted out or sold off, including a hospital, and furniture and construction companies. About 10 percent of ANTEL's 7,052 employees in 1992 were employed in health and security, and over 17 percent were working in non-economic rural offices, some of which generate only 20 colones (US$2.3) a month in revenue.

Like many monopoly carriers, ANTEL generates large revenues for the general budget. It posted earnings of 500 million colones (US$57.8 million) in 1993. But 87 percent of its revenues come from expensive international calls, which in 1991 were 22 to 34 percent more expensive than in other countries in the region. Were the company subjected to greater competition, its sterling financial record would tarnish quickly. Basic telephone rates were not increased for 20 years, and adjustments are made ad hoc to meet cash needs and political objectives. The under-investment that has plagued the sector owes much to recurring government interference. On the strength of its profits the company could have borrowed on capital markets, but it was not permitted to do so. Since 1989, the company has managed with donor support, to upgrade and expand the network. The number of lines doubled to 302,492, or 5.5 lines per 100 inhabitants. About two-thirds of the lines are now digital, and San Salvador has a fiber optic network. But demand for services is racing ahead of supply: the waiting list for lines increased from 162,000 in 1992 to 200,000. ANTEL estimates that by the year 2000 the number of lines would have to rise by 90 percent to catch up on the backlog of orders and accommodate private sector needs.

Reform. Besides stepping up investment, ANTEL's management and the Government have introduced measures since 1989 to increase efficiency. One-time improvements in productivity were achieved partly by cutting staff by about 14 percent over the past three years. Repair response time similarly improved: 90 percent of down lines are now repaired within four days. In addition, ANTEL recently developed a restructuring plan that would divest many non-core activities and public works contracts are increasingly bid out to the private sector. The implementation of turn-key projects by the private sector has helped reduce the project cycle. Time needed for feasibility studies has fallen from 36 to 18 months, and construction from 24 to 18 months. Finally, with IDB support, a review of the legal and institutional framework was completed in February 1994, and with World Bank technical assistance, an action plan was completed in July 1994 for the reform of key public enterprises including ANTEL.

Deepening reform. Modernizing the communications system is critical to the country's export-led growth strategy. It will require large investments in expansion of the basic network; sufficient supply of high-quality fax, data transfer, packet switching, cellular, and other services essential to modern commerce; competition in service delivery to keep prices down; and a regulatory function - clearly separated from telecommunications operations - with responsibility for protecting investors and consumers. These investment requirements can only be met by attracting significant private participation which will require that a clear and credible regulatory regime for entry and prices be established.

Power

Structure. All planning, regulatory and executive functions are vested in the *Comisión Ejecutiva del Rio Lempa* (CEL), a state monopoly. Almost all electric power for public services is generated by CEL (there is a very small amount of self generation), which sells the bulk of its electricity to distribution companies and the remainder to large end-users. In the past, the distribution of electricity (except for rural areas) was in the hands of the private sector through concessions. These expired in 1986, however, and since then four of the seven distribution companies have been under the administration of CEL. The Electric Power Company of El Salvador, formerly one of the private distributors but now controlled by CEL, distributes electricity in the capital area.

Performance. The degree of electrification in El Salvador is low compared to that of other Latin American countries, although access to electricity has increased from 33 percent in 1980 to 61 percent in 1993. Power interruption and voltage irregularities were among the most severe constraints cited in the survey. Although outages have subsided in the past two years, one-third of the survey firms had their own generating capacity, most likely in response to the uncertain power supply. Among large enterprises, 55 percent had their own capacity. During the 1980s CEL entered into a period of prolonged decline. During the civil war there were over 2,000 attacks on substations and 3,800 on the transmission system costing CEL about US$200 million. Moreover, during the last decade there was significant government intervention in setting tariffs. Rates were not based on economic criteria, and CEL was not allowed to make automatic adjustments for inflation, devaluation or other cost increases. By the end of the decade the average tariff was 33 percent of long run marginal cost (LRMC). In the early 1990s a prolonged drought required CEL to purchase energy from Guatemala and to increase fuel purchases to substitute for hydro power. These events strained the already weakened capacity of CEL, and as a consequence power interruptions and voltage fluctuations became frequent. Although, the situation is improving, the capacity of CEL to meet demand is inadequate. Demand grew by about 10 percent p.a. during 1991-93 immediately following the peace accord, and is expected to grow at 9 percent p.a. through the end of the decade. The power sector now faces an enormous backlog of investment.

Reform. The power sector has been a high Government priority and significant progress has been achieved. In May 1991 the Government adopted an Energy Sector Policy consistent with an open, market-based economy. It set four objectives: (i) an appropriate legal and institutional framework; (ii) adoption of pricing policies based on economic costs; (iii) significant private sector participation; and (iv) establishment of an institutional and policy framework to address environmental issues. A package of energy legislation establishing planning and regulatory agencies, a framework for power tariffs and a corporatized CEL has been submitted to the Assembly. The first independent power generation project (80 MW) was announced in October 1993. The Government has also decided to re-privatize power distribution. CEL's efficiency has been high in spite of the events of the last decade. Compared to other Central American countries, CEL has the highest number of customers per employee and ranks second in energy sales per employee. A tariff increase of 32 percent was applied in late 1992, and the Government has further committed to reach 85 percent of LRMC by 1996 and 100 percent by 1999.

Deepening reform. The critical next step is to establish a track record of implementation of the necessary policy and institutional reforms. Significant additional tariff increases are required to reach the 85 percent of LRMC goal in 1996. New concessions need to be granted for private power distributors. Additional independent power projects are planned for 1995 (80 MW) and 1997 (50 MW). Implicit in the new structure of the sector is a re-shaped role for CEL, partitioned between generation and transmission, with each organized as an independent commercial enterprise. In the future CEL-Generation would generate power, buy it from independent power producers through power purchase arrangements, or compete directly with them to supply energy to large consumers or distribution companies. CEL-Transmission would retain its central role in power transmission but would be established as an independent company and guarantee open access to generators. CEL's current activities in urban power distribution would effectively cease with the sale of its current franchises to private operators.

Roads

Structure. The Ministry of Public Works (MOP) is responsible for the transport sector. The Vice Ministry of Public Works is responsible for highway maintenance, rehabilitation and construction, through the *Dirección General de Caminos* (national roads) and *Dirección de Urbanismo y Arquitectura* (urban roads). Municipalities have responsibility for portions of the urban road network.

Performance. El Salvador has approximately 12,400 kms of roads: (i) 1,936 kms paved with 38 percent in bad condition, 30 percent in fair condition, and 32 percent in good conditions; (ii) 7,890 kms unpaved with 57 percent in bad condition, 31 percent in fair condition, 12 percent in good condition (iii) 112 kms in San Salvador (fair to good condition); and (iv) other municipalities, 2,474 kms in generally bad condition. The primary road network consists of two East-West axes, the Panamerican Highway and the Coastal Highway, and four North-South axes. Supply of roads and highways is sufficient, except for rural penetration roads in the ex-conflict areas. However, deficiencies in the transport sector were the most severe infrastructure constraint noted in the survey. Maintenance suffers from under-execution and inefficiencies and salaries and benefits comprise about 80 percent of the road maintenance budget.

Reform. A Vice Ministry of Transport has recently been established to direct and coordinate policy. It will assume functions that were previously handled by other ministries (transport regulation, user fees and tolls), eventually becoming the transport regulatory authority. In parallel a number of regulatory actions have been taken (establishing weight limits and facilitating border crossings), and a number of institutional changes in MOP have been initiated. Staff levels in the MOP have been reduced significantly, particularly in the *Dirección General de Caminos*.

Deepening reform. Improving the quality of existing roads through increased maintenance, rehabilitation and modernization is the principal challenge. MOP has prepared a five year rehabilitation and maintenance plan but it must secure budget allocations for road maintenance over the long term. Funds are assigned to MOP as part of the central government's budget process, based on last year's level of expenditures with no analysis or evaluation of programs. Moreover, there is a bias toward external funds which, however, are for discrete programs with defined time frames. Ideally they can supplement but not substitute for long term road maintenance funds.

Ports and Rail

Structure. The *Comisión Ejecutiva Portuaria Autónoma* (CEPA) has responsibility for the ports of Acajutla and Cutuco, the state owned railroad and the airport. CEPA was created in 1952 to manage Acajutla, and added responsibilities during the 1970s. Planning, regulatory and executive functions are vested in CEPA, although with significant intervention from line ministries.

Performance. Acajutla is an open access port on the Pacific Coast about 85 kms southwest of San Salvador. It has capacity for about 1,500 million metric tons, and is close to reaching that level, with total traffic of about 1,300 million metric tons in 1993. Cutuco, also on the Pacific coast about 185 kms from San Salvador, handled 50,00 tons in 1991, one-fifth of its 1978 traffic level. The railroad is severely deteriorated with 50 percent of its sleepers damaged. Rolling stock is in a similarly deteriorated state. CEPA estimates that only 2 percent of the nation's cargo traffic moves by rail. The airport dates from 1978, has a small role in exporting (about 1 percent of all exports), but is increasingly important in non-traditional exports. CEPA is relatively stable financially. It earns a modest profit due to airport operations, while the railroad loses money and the ports break even. Acajutla suffers from labor and operational problems, which leads to a lack of competitiveness with some other Central American ports. Labor concessions in the 1980s have led to a salary structure and work rules that are increasingly constraining CEPA's competitiveness. The most important competition is from Puerto Queztal in Guatemala. Additionally the lack of maintenance and investment during the 1980s created a backlog at Acajutla that is slowly being addressed by CEPA. Cutuco has limited installations, is only accessible by railroad, and must compete with the nearby privately owned port of Punta Gorda.

Reform. The Government has initiated a number of changes and is actively exploring privatization options, including granting operating concessions, divesting storage facilities and contracting out maintenance. CEPA has improved its financial situation through tariff increases and has taken steps to reduce personnel at Acajutla by about half (650 out of 1,400 workers).

Deepening reform. Although CEPA has achieved financial stability and is improving efficiency, it faces a number of strategic issues. It must recover traffic lost during the civil war and compete, in price and services, with Central American ports. This will require greater private sector participation, and the transformation of CEPA into a regulatory authority.

Water and Sanitation

Structure. The *Administración Nacional de Acueductos y Alcantarillados* (ANDA) is the principal water and sanitation institution, but responsibilities are spread across many institutions. Water/sanitation production and distribution is split between ANDA for most urban systems, some municipalities, and the Ministry of Health for rural systems. The Social Investment Fund (FIS) also participates in the construction of rural systems.

Performance. All water produced in El Salvador is sub-surface. For the most part rivers and lakes are too contaminated for use. Water coverage was 55 percent in 1992, of which 78 percent was urban and 16 percent rural. Sanitation coverage was 69 percent, of which 87 percent was urban and 52 percent latrines. There are ten waste water treatment plants but these handle only 3 percent of production. Demand is projected to grow at 4 percent p.a. through the end of the decade. To reach 100 percent coverage in the municipalities covered by ANDA, investments on the order of US$150 million p.a. would be needed over the next five years. Losses are estimated at 40 percent and service is intermittent. In San Salvador it was estimated in 1993 that users received water about 16-18 hours per day. Of the

350,000 connections, about two-thirds have working meters. ANDA's financial problems are largely the result of the tariff structure, as well as weaknesses in its billing and collection systems.

Reform. Some initial steps have been taken toward sectoral reform. A draft diagnostic study of the water/sanitation sector has been prepared and new draft legislation is currently under review. In the last five years ANDA has been able to improve its financial situation. Operating losses have been reduced by about two-thirds, and the overall deficit by about one-third. Tariff increases in 1990 and 1992 contributed to the improved financial performance.

Deepening reform. The Government must implement tariff reform, and address simultaneously the rehabilitation and expansion of production and distribution systems. Establishment of planning and regulatory agencies is essential. The Government lacks a water resources strategy and policies for conservation and usage. Too little attention is given to environmental issues, especially in view of the decline in aquifers and the low coverage of waste water. The institutional framework is disjointed, and there is a multiplicity of institutions operating in an uncoordinated and ineffective fashion.

CHAPTER IV

MODERNIZING THE LEGAL AND REGULATORY FRAMEWORK

Laws and regulations and their proper enforcement are essential in facilitating competitive markets and defining the rules of the game. Uniform and clear interpretation of the laws leads to lower transaction costs and increased economic activity. In El Salvador many business laws are outdated and impose burdensome requirements, mainly related to the conditions for doing business (commercial code, foreign investment law, bankruptcy law, and competition law). To a lesser extent, laws related to property rights and the mechanism of their transfer (contracts) could benefit from revision. Poor application and enforcement also adversely affects private sector activities. To improve international competitiveness and increase economic activity and private sector development, the legal and regulatory framework needs to be revised. Reforms should focus on: establishing and securing property rights; improving contract law; facilitating company entry, operation, and exit; strengthening competition policy and consumer protection; eliminating tax distortions and disincentives; and improving enforcement capacity and judicial institutions.

ESTABLISHING AND SECURING PROPERTY RIGHTS

Real property. Property rights over land and other durable goods should be secure so as to allow them to be used as credit collateral and encourage land owners to make investments. This is achieved through effective real property registration systems. Property rights are well defined in El Salvador and the only limits on ownership are for rural real property exceeding 245 hectares. However, there are issues related to backlogged and inefficient registration, and lengthy resolution of conflicts.

The Registry of Real Property (*Registro de la Propriedad Raíz e Hipotecas [RPRH]*), a department of the Ministry of Justice, records all rights and real property contracts. Registration is manual and in some cases can take more than a year. In addition, the process of securing information is lengthy and unreliable, mostly due to inconsistencies between cadastre (handled by the *Instituto Geográfico Nacional [IGN]* a Directorate of the Ministry of Public Works) and land registry information. The Government is currently initiating a pilot program in Sonsonate, with World Bank support, to improve the land registry and cadastre services. Currently any land conflict must be resolved in Court; the Government, is preparing proposals for alternative dispute resolution methods to solve conflicts related to registration and cadastral matters. To modernize and improve the efficiency of RPRH: (i) combine land registry and cadastre information in single records in one institution under the Ministry of Justice; (ii) carry out a national area-based land registry and cadastral updating; (iii) computerize and decentralize data to facilitate access; and (iv) develop and implement alternative extra-judicial dispute resolution methods.

Intellectual property rights. Effective protection of intellectual property rights (IPR) (patents, trademarks, copyrights) is essential for technological innovation and technology transfer. Registration and filing are usual prerequisites for acquiring, transferring and protecting a right. A revised IPR law was enacted in August 1993, but institutional and enforcement shortcomings still exist. Trademark and copyright piracy is a serious problem (there is not much experience of patents), which discourages national and foreign investors. More specifically, IPR protection is handicapped by delays in registration and weak enforcement. The *Registro de Comercio* is excessively slow: up to 3 years to register a trademark and up to 5 years to file a patent. As of early 1994, there was a backlog of almost 2,000 unregistered trademarks with only three people processing them. Penalties for IPR infringement are not large. In copyright cases, criminal penalties are greater than civil ones, but fines are not a strong deterrent. Furthermore, the aggrieved parties have to seek protection through the courts, which is slow and inefficient. Litigation involves sophisticated issues, where the poor training of the judiciary leads to unpredictable outcomes and lengthy delays.

To fight piracy and to improve IPR protection: (i) increase the fee for the filing of a patent, trademark, or copyright to finance office technology upgrading and additional staff; (ii) combine civil (filing claims) and ex-officio enforcement by the Competition Policies Agency; (iii) create a specialized administrative agency to register, supervise and police the market, which could also act as the administrative forum (at least of first instance) for the adjudication of claims; (iv) provide for regional offices; and (v) revise legal remedies and set stricter penalties.

IMPROVING CONTRACT LAW

Contracts set business rules between parties and provide the mechanism for transferring property rights. In El Salvador contract law is contained in the Civil Code. Contract rules do not appear to impose limitations on contracting, although the relevant Civil Code provisions date from 1860. However, there is a need to better define: (i) extra-contractual responsibilities, which are narrow and outdated in comparison with real-life claims; and (ii) guidelines for calculation of damages (which are non-existent). Although assessing extra-contractual claims is always complicated and can be arbitrary, guidelines should be developed to make court awards more predictable.

FACILITATING COMPANY ENTRY, OPERATION, AND EXIT

Registration process. Entry appears to be reasonably free, although it is time consuming and costly. Currently 14 laws regulate the registration process, which requires 16 forms to be submitted and 32 visits to different institutions. This makes the process slow, complex, costly and constitutes a disincentive to formalize. Mandatory steps take approximately 40 days while additional special ones take approximately one week. Registration time and costs are not high when compared to other Latin American countries that have not reformed the registry process, but are quite high when compared to countries that have done so (Chile, Colombia, Uruguay and Peru).

To address this constraint a one-stop-window (*Proyecto de la Ventanilla Unica*) administered by the *Oficina Nacional de Inversiones* (ONI) began to operate in mid-1994. Originally envisaged to facilitate foreign investment, ONI also handles domestic investors. It is expected to significantly streamline registration since it encompasses the whole process and nullifies any legal inconsistencies. However, a number of additional steps should be considered:

⇨ *centralize the institutional structure*: ONI was conceived as a department of the Ministry of Economy (MOE) to assume full responsibility for all registration of national and foreign investment and reduce duplication. In that event, registration at the *Registro de Comercio* (RDC - under the Ministry of Justice) would have been eliminated. However, it appears that ONI will start functioning under the MOE and will transfer all documents to the Ministry of Justice. This will relieve the investor from having to visit different offices but will not change core procedures;

⇨ *assess the purpose and value of remaining steps*: while the one-stop-window has accelerated the approval process the number of steps remains the same. There is still room to streamline registration by eliminating unnecessary steps. The requirements imposed by the 1973 *Ley de Registro de Comercio* and the 1973 *Ley de la Superintendencia de Sociedades y Empresas Mercantiles*, sometimes include the submission of the same documents to different authorities. For example, one authorization permit is needed from the RDC qualifying the businessman (with a copy to the Superintendencia*)*, and another for the company and each of its locations. In addition, many requirements set in the *Superintendencia de Sociedades* (SS) are outdated and need to be revised. For example, a company with assets equivalent to 10,000 colones (US$1,200) needs to have its accounting system authorized before it can start operations; and

⇨ *further streamline microenterprise registration*: microenterprises are subject to procedures similar to those that apply to other enterprises. For example, all enterprises including microenterprises need to renew their operation permits annually at the RDC by submitting their balance sheets.

To further simplify and speed the registration process: (i) promote the autonomy of MOE in the ONI project, making it solely responsible for registration; (ii) reduce or eliminate the notification/publication requirement; (iii) enact simplified rules for the registration of microenterprises, setting a 'one-stop, one-day' window for their registration, as successfully used in Peru; (iv) computerize RDC; and (v) institute time limitations for licenses and other approvals.

Supervision of companies. The SS has a national staff of 17 auditors and two desktop computers. In addition to the workload from San Salvador, it also deals with documents from all regional offices, which simply receive documents and do not act. To strengthen the supervision of companies: (i) create one entity to register and supervise; (ii) replace a priori controls with ex post verification by a strong and competent authority. For example, the accounting system needs to be authorized by SS and legalized by RDC, which could be replaced by strict ex post verification; (iii) provide SS with resources to assume a more dynamic role in information and supervision; and (iv) strengthen regional offices.

Commercial Code provisions. A number of unnecessary procedures in the Commercial Code should be eliminated, such as: (i) to renew operating permits, all firms have to submit balance sheets and performance results annually, whether they are microenterprises or incorporated societies; (ii) all installment contracts for the sale of movable durables have to be registered; (iii) all credit contracts for production (quite broadly defined) have to be registered; (iv) there are unwarranted restrictions on the maximum term for production credit contracts (Art.1149); (v) there is an urgent need to revise and simplify the list of items subject to the Commercial Registry (Arts. 3-7, Chapter II, Commercial Registry Law), which are mostly unneccesary; and (vi) similar unnecessary burdens appear in a number of other areas such as the *Solvencias Municipales,* health permits for foodstuff producers, and the requirement that VAT filings be signed and submitted only by the head of the company.

To simplify the Commercial Code: (i) require renewal of annual operation permits only by incorporated enterprises that have a fiduciary responsibility to their shareholders. All other companies should submit documents every five years, with the exception of microenterprises, which should be exempt; (ii) set a threshold to exempt goods from the sale registry; and (iii) eliminate unnecessary procedures and restrictions built into the Commercial Code and Commercial Registry. A small *Comité de Desburocratización* should be set-up with responsibility for eliminating unnecessary procedures, and consolidating the remainder (as used in Uruguay with great success and at a very low cost). It should ask the private sector for suggestions for the reduction of investigation costs.

Foreign investment rules. Foreign investors still face a number of procedural and structural entry barriers, and a number of sectoral restrictions,[1] although a more liberal foreign investment regulation was enacted in 1988. In addition to the requirements described above for Salvadoran companies, a foreign company needs to be registered with MOE.[2] The company has to prove

---

[1] The Constitution prohibits FDI in rural real property; certain fishing activities; and "small" commerce, industry, and services.

[2] Registration of foreign investment is not mandatory. However, in practice most foreign investors register in order to be eligible for tax credits for dividends and reinvested profits, and to be able to remit dividends and repatriate capital.

compliance with the minimum capital requirements for foreign investment, and SS has discretion in establishing the minimum capital of the foreign company, which can be higher but not lower than the amount imposed by the law. Once authorization has been obtained from the Ministry of Justice in the form of an executive agreement, it has to be legalized by the Ministry of Foreign Affairs and registered at the Commercial Registry. Another license for commerce and industry has to be obtained from the Commercial Registry, which seems to overlap with the authorization referred to above. Requirements are even more onerous for the establishment of a foreign subsidiary. In addition, the FDI legal regime does not provide guarantees relating to national treatment and protection against expropriation. The Law should be amended to: (i) modify the onerous provisions of the SS and the LRC; (ii) eliminate the SS foreign investment requirement - and its discretion - defining minimum capital; and (iii) reduce to one the authorizations required by the Ministry of Justice and the Commercial Registry.

Exit: bankruptcy and liquidation. Fast and efficient bankruptcy proceedings are an important mechanism to protect creditors and facilitate the reallocation of resources. The key objective is to maximize the value of assets under bankruptcy through reorganization or liquidation. In El Salvador bankruptcy proceedings are cumbersome and practically never used. They are set in the 1973 *Ley de Procedimientos Mercantiles,* which is drafted in the spirit that companies will resist going out of business. On the one hand, going out of business is considered more difficult than entering the market; even companies in great financial distress prefer abandoning the company to filing for bankruptcy. On the other hand, creditors prefer to execute their secured rights through the courts rather than initiate bankruptcy proceedings. Thus, all creditors require first mortgages to secure credits. Proceedings are lengthy and there are no alternatives to judicial declaration of bankruptcy, such as extra-judicial declaration and reorganization. Additional constraints include: (i) costly procedures; (ii) criminal implications of bankruptcy if debts are not paid; and (iii) insufficient processing capacity and expertise in the court system.

To provide guarantees to creditors for the protection of their rights, as well as to allow flexible allocation of resources, the law should be revised to: (i) allow for speedy proceedings by imposing time limits at different stages; and (ii) introduce alternatives for defaulting debtors, offering flexibility to insolvent companies. Business reorganization would allow continued operation under court supervision - if there was hope of recovery - until a reorganization plan was approved by creditors.

STRENGTHENING COMPETITION POLICY AND CONSUMER PROTECTION

Unfair competition appears to be a serious problem in El Salvador. Survey results show that 59 percent of firms experienced problems with informal or illegal competition. It was most common in commerce, where 74 percent of firms identified the problem. The key concerns where: evasion of the VAT and other taxes; firms selling below cost; avoidance of trade and customs regulations; avoidance of labor regulations and taxes; and anti-competitive practices. A Consumer Protection Law was enacted in 1992, but questions remain on its focus and enforcement.

Article 110 of the Constitution prohibits monopolistic practices, but there is no complementary enacted law or enforcement of any sort against that kind of practice. There is a need for a comprehensive antitrust policy and for its proper enforcement:

⇨ *price fixing and other agreements, cartels and geographical market segmentation:* examples appear in: beer, advertising agencies, radio and TV, airlines, pharmacies, hardware stores, financial institutions, hotels, milk, and distribution of basic products. The welfare loss from collusive practices can be quite significant, yet no effort is being made to discourage or punish them. The legislation in this area is deficient and needs revisions;

⇨ *smuggling, and tax and social security (ISSS) payments evasion:* the loss of economic activity caused by smuggling is quite significant in some sectors (shoes, textiles, liquor, cigarettes and some durable goods). Tax and ISSS payments evasion provide an unfair competitive advantage by lowering the costs of the offenders relative to those of the compliers, and increases the fiscal burden on the tax compliers. Apparently a number of firms, while registered, do not pay ISSS taxes; and

⇨ *procurement and government contracts:* while improvements have been achieved, there are apparently valid complains of more than occasional lack of transparency and competitive bidding.

The Government should enact a modern competition policy and antitrust law addressing monopolistic practices and restraints of trade agreements. It should treat any agreement among competitors as illegal per se, as well as some vertical restrictions such as tie-ins and resale price maintenance. Other anti-competitive practices should be treated under the rule of reason. In addition, although the Consumer Protection Law is adequate, it should be streamlined and the focus sharpened as a secondary priority. To strengthen enforcement, the Government should create an autonomous enforcement agency with investigative and judicial powers, albeit in separate commissions and in parallel to the proposed new competition legislation. The present *Dirección General de Protección al Consumidor* could be restructured into this type of agency, with jurisdiction over both activities. In fact, it would be desirable to have a single agency responsible for enforcing antitrust, consumer protection and intellectual property law and trade policies. It could be modeled along the lines of the Peruvian INDECOPY agency. The complementarity among these themes and the scarcity of qualified staff would make such institutional arrangement ideal, capturing synergism and enhancing on-the-job learning. The main focus should shift from consumer protection to agreements of all types among competitors and restraint of trade issues, where welfare losses are larger. It should also increase efforts by agencies dealing with smuggling and tax evasion, increase penalties, and improve the inspection system.

ELIMINATING TAX DISTORTIONS AND DISINCENTIVES[3]

Addressing distorted incentives. The 1992 income tax law has simplified company income taxation and eliminated some of the allocative distortions of the previous statute. Additional steps should be taken to eliminate the differentiations in treatment of various types of financial instruments, with respect to each other, or with respect to other forms of income. Currently: (i) interest from Government and Central Bank bonds is exempt from taxes, which introduces a tax wedge between public and private debt instruments, and the existence of taxable and tax exempt private bonds discriminates between private institutions; (ii) income from loans made by foreign-based banks is exempt from taxes, while income from loans by national banks is subject to income tax; and (iii) all financial instruments traded in the stock exchange and held by persons are tax exempt. This discriminates in favor of the stock exchange and against other financial institutions. In addition, eliminate VAT's differential treatment of the stock exchange and commercial banks. The latter are exempt from levying the VAT on the fees associated with lending to a corporation. In contrast, the sale of a corporate bond in the stock exchange gives rise to a VAT on the commission charged, raising borrowing costs through the stock exchange relative to commercial banks.

Controlling unfair competition. Evasion of the three major taxes - the VAT, customs, and the income tax - and of employment taxes are stated to prevail in all sectors. Evasion is singled out as a

---

[3] As discussed in Chapter II, the tax system rests on income taxes (personal and corporate), import duties, and VAT. Businesses also pay employment taxes and municipal taxes. The former consist of social security contributions of 7.5 percent, contributions to the social housing fund of 5 percent, and professional training institute charges of 1 percent. The cost of labor is thereby raised by 13.5 percent, assuming these labor charges are absorbed by the employer and not shifted back onto wages and salaries. Municipal taxes are levied on the assets of the corporations and are a deductible cost. In 1992 they were estimated to amount to around 28 million colones which represent about 4 percent of the corporate income tax yield of that year.

significant factor especially in trade (particularly at the retail level), but also in industry, and for all sizes of enterprises. Some firms evade the income tax by simply not registering which also leads to non-compliance with payroll taxes. The evasion of the VAT and customs duties is singled out particularly in the leather goods industry, pharmaceutical products, and in machinery and equipment (especially electronic appliances). Smuggling of imported goods apparently continues to prevail despite the reductions in tariffs. To control unfair competition and corruption the Government should consider: (i) easing the administrative process; reducing the need to resort to higher echelons; eliminating corruption in the tax and legal systems through civil service reform; (ii) reducing smuggling; and (iii) reforming and strengthening municipal tax administration.

Diminishing compliance costs. Administrative procedures are deemed burdensome, but especially in VAT and tax and customs administration. Although the VAT is assumed to finally rest on the final consumer and, therefore, is not a direct cost for businesses, it carries relatively high compliance costs, since it involves sophisticated book-keeping and a great number of transactions in recording debits and credits. In addition, the fiscal credit of the VAT should legally be refunded within 3 months but takes longer than a year. Finally, tax and customs administration is heavily bureaucratic, complicated, and time consuming, hence costly. The administrative system contains a number of loopholes which make it inefficient and leave room for evasion and corruption. Its modernization is a top priority. To diminish compliance costs the Government should: (i) streamline regulations and simplify and expedite procedures, particularly payments and refunds; (ii) implement cross-referencing; (ii) improve customs administration; and (iii) consider the privatization of customs administration to reduce corruption and broaden the tax base.

IMPROVING ENFORCEMENT CAPACITY AND JUDICIAL INSTITUTIONS

Addressing court-related issues. For disputes regarding non-mainstream contract breaches the main issue is predictability. The Commercial Code is silent on a number of important areas and grants judges discretion to look for commercial custom when adjudicating cases in those areas. In practice, judges are timid and uncomfortable with commercial transactions not expressly mentioned in the Code. This leads to unpredictable and often arbitrary outcomes, due mostly to lack of exposure and knowledge of the new instruments and arrangements being introduced. There is also an issue related to the lack of functional autonomy; excessive power is concentrated in the Supreme Court, which regulates practically everything. It appoints judges and exercises disciplinary authority over notaries and lawyers. While it pronounces on the constitutionality of laws and executive actions, at the same time it acts as the forum of last resort for the adjudication of claims. However, instead of providing guidance by its jurisprudence, it has consistently abstained from any substantive interpretation of laws and has merely focused on legalisms. Finally, procedures for civil actions contained in the 1857 Civil Procedure Code are outdated.

Fostering alternative dispute resolution mechanisms. Alternative dispute resolution mechanisms (such as arbitration, conciliation and mediation) are neither well known nor used. Such mechanisms could increase predictability, reduce costs to the parties and provide better chances of enforcement. Although the Civil Procedure Code and Commercial Code permit arbitration, their use is inhibited by cumbersome procedures, lack of awareness of their existence, and obligation to conduct arbitration in court. To increase the predictability and speed of conflict resolution and enforcement of laws and regulations: (i) set up a bar association to supervise and discipline lawyers and notaries, and introduce public examination for the selection of judges; (ii) revise the 1857 Civil Procedure Code to introduce oral proceedings and to review terms of law suits; and (iii) provide commercial judges with education and more training on new commercial transactions. Seminars and conferences on recent financing developments would provide much needed information and understanding of this growing area. To foster use of arbitration undertake research to determine the most appropriate arbitration mechanisms, and in the interim, revise the arbitration law to reduce intervention by the courts and to make arbitration more accessible. An arbitration forum could also be created. Finally, to reform procedures for commercial dispute resolution a comprehensive review of the following areas should be undertaken: (i) court procedures costs, including an estimation of foregone credit opportunities due to creditors' lack of confidence in enforcement; (ii) laws governing court procedures; and (iii) the practical side of court procedures for commercial dispute resolution, including an identification of unnecessary and time-consuming steps, and of formal arbitration laws.

CHAPTER V

FACILITATING TRADE AND TECHNOLOGICAL DIFFUSION

To meet the challenge of globalization El Salvador must improve policies and structures to support outward-oriented growth. It should continue ensuring a friendly environment for trade and address technology constraints which limit productivity and international competitiveness. Trade reforms have been impressive and accompanied by increased private sector efforts to adapt to new market conditions. Results are promising, but further efforts are needed to ensure the sustainability of trade reforms and fully remove constraints to the expansion and diversification of exports. A stable macroeconomic environment and the removal of constraints to private sector development will be key, but parallel efforts are necessary to eliminate remaining policy and institutional obstacles to trade expansion and to support technological diffusion.

TRADE POLICY: DEEPENING AND SUSTAINING LIBERALIZATION

Moving to a uniform tariff rate. Since 1989, tariffs have been reduced from 0-290 percent to 5-20 percent and the number of rates from 25 to 3. The Government announced in February 1995 the lowering of tariffs on capital goods to 1 percent and a schedule for further reductions which is being discussed with the Central American Common Market (CACM). Coefficients of variation and unweighted means have also been significantly lowered. However, tariff dispersion is still high and the structure still reflects significant trade biases. For example, producers of final agriculture manufactured products enjoy levels of protection higher than producers of agriculture inputs. To eliminate dispersion and lower evasion, the Government should consider moving to a uniform tariff rate.

Table V.1 Tariff Structure, 1988-94

Year	No. of Tariff Rates	Tariff Range
Before Sept. 1989	25	0-290
September 1989 a/	9	1, 5, 10, 20, 25, 30, 35, 40, and 50
April 1990 a/	6	5, 10, 20, 25, 30, and 35
June 1991 b/	5	5, 10, 20, 25, and 30
December 1991 b/	4	5, 10, 20, and 25
March 1992 a/	5	5, 10, 20, 25 and 30
December 1994 a/	3	5, 10, and 20

Proposed reforms announced February 1995:

1995	1% on Capital Goods
1996	1-15
1997	1-12
1998	1-9
1999	1-6

a/ Including Part III.   b/ Excluding Part III.
Sources: Compilation of legislations provided by GAES/MIPLAN.

Eliminating remaining administrative instruments regulating import flows. Although remaining NTBs cover less than 5 percent of all tariff lines, administrative regulations on imports still exist. At the root of the problem are laws[1] which regulate remaining import permits and cause considerable overlap in administrative procedures. Draft decrees modifying these four laws were submitted to the Assembly in late 1994, but have not yet been approved.

Responding to the challenge of NAFTA. There is uncertainty regarding the impact of NAFTA on the Salvadoran export sector. Nevertheless, NAFTA adds urgency to the need to increase global competitivenss, rather than waiting for the granting of preferential access. While there are on-going discussions on the possible granting of NAFTA parity to the Central America region, it is clear that

---

[1]   *Ley de Sanidad Agropecuaria*; the Health Code; the *Ley de Farmacia* (6/30/1927); and Decree No. 647.

economies such as El Salvador will face increasing competition for foreign investment and trade, particularily in clothing and textiles. However, a recent study concludes that El Salvador could benefit from NAFTA, provided it can access the Mexican market, which has great incentives to divert its production to the higher-priced US market (Leamer and others, 1995).

REMOVING EXPORT-SPECIFIC CONSTRAINTS

The Government can enhance export supply response by acting in three policy areas:

⇨ **ensuring a stable macroeconomic environment** (Chapter II);

⇨ **removing general constraints which lower productivity and affect all private firms** through the implementation of reforms to improve human and physical infrastructure (Chapter III), modernize the business environment (Chapter IV) and strengthen the financial sector (Chapter VI); and

⇨ **removing export-specific constraints**, through a distortion-correction approach to export promotion. This approach is the most consistent with optimal trade policy theory, policy experience, and political economy considerations.[2] To have a positive impact, export development policies should be designed to address in a non-targeted, universal fashion, export-specific public sector management issues and microeconomic non-price supply side constraints at the firm level.

Despite reforms implemented since 1989, a number of policies and administrative mechanisms impede the achievement of policy neutrality between domestic and international markets and negatively influence export competitiveness. These constraints include: (i) lengthy, complicated, and non-transparent import procedures; (ii) export-related administrative and institutional weaknesses; (iii) inadequate support for technology diffusion and product quality; (iv) weak trade negotiation capabilities; and (v) weak government-business interaction.

Addressing import-related issues

Lengthy, complicated, and non-transparent import procedures are the most important remaining obstacles to trade. Survey results show that import duties and other import taxes are perceived by the private sector to be moderately high. However, other import costs, such as services of customs brokers and special payments, add a substantial margin to the cost of importing, not counting the time lost by bureaucratic red tape which is mentioned as a not insignificant obstacle. This margin adds 3 percentage points to the cost of importing in manufacturing, trade, and constructions and 5 percentage points in services, and rises with the size of the enterprise.

To further reduce import-related administrative costs the Government should:

⇨ **establish a one-stop window for imports,** along the lines of the existing export-processing center (para. 5.10): the issuance of import licenses by the MOE is discretionary and document processing by the Treasury and the Court of Accounts is lengthy and cumbersome; and

⇨ **accelerate on-going customs reforms:** the most time consuming procedures are document verification, acquiring a customs certificate, and merchandise valuation processes. The Government's ongoing customs administration reforms should be accelerated.

---

[2] Recent developments in trade theory (the "new trade theory") suggest an active Government role in trade policy, particularly support to specific export activities. Its relevance to developing countries has been questioned. Support to specific activities can be accommodated within a framework of distortion-correction, but only after a number of fundamental export promotion conditions are satisfied (including the maintenance of macroeconomic stability and the adoption of policies to offset the anti-export bias). In addition, specific support should be at the initiative of the private sector, subject to evaluation as an investment in knowledge, and should be time-bound (Rajapatirana, 1993).

Addressing export-related administrative and institutional weaknesses

In addition to tariff and NTB reduction, the Government has reduced the anti-export bias by: (i) simplifying export administrative procedures through the creation in 1989 of a one-stop export processing center (CENTREX) in the Central Bank; (ii) introducing a regime for free trade zones (FTZs) and Fiscal Areas; and (iii) adopting a duty drawback system. However, administrative and institutional weaknesses persist and a number of additional steps should be considered.

Improving CENTREX. Public sector support services for foreign trade activities are weak. Survey results indicated that firms use special agents to facilitate procedures and that, in addition to devoting around 10 percent of their time to solving procedural problems, firm costs due to institutional obstacles may go up to 4 percent of the CIF import value. The establishment of CENTREX was an important step, but a CENTREX survey suggests that its operations could be further improved. The processing period is still long and the documents delivery date is typically not honored; the rationale behind application rejections is not transparent, making it difficult to comply with requirements. The survey also suggests that users would like the Center to operate on Saturdays and in other areas such as Santa Ana and San Miguel. Users would be willing to be charged for these services.

Improving the functioning of FTZs and Fiscal Areas. One of the main objectives of the new development strategy is to move the whole economy toward a free trade regime. In the interim, the Government should further streamline FTZs and Fiscal Areas procedures, and establish a one-stop window for both. The Government promotes nontraditional exports through a regulatory framework embodied in the 1990 FTZs and Fiscal Areas Law and in the Law to Reactivate Exports, which aim to reduce the anti-export bias created by restrictions on trade. The schemes grant tax benefits such as exemptions from income tax, import duties, VAT, and the net wealth tax to extra-regional non-traditional exports. Although there has been some recent improvement, the schemes do not work well and product leakages to the domestic market are frequent.

FTZs and Fiscal Areas are growing productive sectors of the economy thanks to the combination of: (i) duty-free access to the US market of products assembled using components produced in the US; (ii) good quality products; and (iii) competitive wages. The only public FTZ is currently being privatized. Private investment in FTZ and Fiscal Areas amounted to US$25.6 million in 1993 (FUSADES). Operating FTZs do not have room for new firms and the Government has allowed new firms to operate in the Fiscal Areas enjoying the same incentives as FTZ firms. There are 20 firms in FTZs and 161 firms in Fiscal Areas.

The FTZ and Fiscal Areas scheme does not operate satisfactorily. An MOE survey confirmed that the main bottlenecks are: (i) complicated, non-transparent registration procedures;[3] (ii) discretionary practices in customs; the fiscal and customs controls are done by the Treasury Department, but Customs officials may contest the classification of an import even though it has already been authorized by MOE; (iii) lack of adequate infrastructure; and (iv) complicated immigration procedures. To help eliminate these bottlenecks the Government has established an office to support foreign investors (*Oficina de Apoyo al Inversionista Extranjero*), complementing private efforts to attract foreign investment.

Addressing duty drawback-related issues. The Law to Reactivate Exports grants exports of goods (with the exception of coffee, sugar, and cotton) and services to countries outside the CACM a rebate of 6 percent of their f.o.b. value (for goods) and of their invoice value (for services), for duties

---

[3] Steps include: (i) present qualification documentation including a feasibility study to the MOE; (ii) present application documentation to the MOE; (iii) present the statutes of the FTZ to the MOE; (iv) MOE inspects the zone; and (v) MOE approves or rejects project.

paid on imported products utilized in their production. The drawback is also extended to the domestic value added content of assembly or "maquila" operations. These export operations are also exempt from the net wealth tax in proportion to the share of exports within total production, or in the case of assembly operations, in proportion to the domestic value added of exports.

Despite recent improvements, the scheme has a number of weaknesses:

⇨ Delays in obtaining the rebate are the most important regulatory constraint for firms that export more than 25 percent of their production. Currently, the rebate period is around 65 days for the import duty and 50 days for the value-added (compared with the 45 day maximum period stipulated by law). Delays are due to the many steps and Government agencies involved in processing the rebate request: the Central Bank and Customs issue several export documents; the Ministry of Finance receives the rebate application; the MOE reviews the application; the Ministry of Finance reviews the MOE evaluation; the Corte de Cuentas reviews the Ministry of Finance evaluation and gives clearance; and finally, the Treasury issues the rebate;

⇨ It discriminates among regional and extra-regional markets, since the rebates apply only to exports outside the CACM region and it discriminates among products, in that it only applies to exports of non-traditional items;

⇨ It is a single average rate that does not take into account the structural differences among industries. A single average rate facilitates its administration and makes it easier to determine and control its magnitude, but it does not assure that the drawback actually corresponds to the duties paid on imported inputs by a particular exporter;[4] and

⇨ The VAT, because of its fiscal credit mechanism, eliminates the indirect taxes on inputs used in export production and extends it to indirect inputs as well. Thus the import duty rebate cum VAT reduces the cost of exports with reference to taxes. This, however, does not totally eliminate problems of resource allocation, since duty free import of inputs for the production of exported goods discriminates against similar inputs produced domestically if their prices are duty inclusive.[5]

In the medium-term, the drawback should be eliminated as El Salvador moves toward a freer trade system. To continue with the drawback system will imply transfers to exporters from other taxpayers. In the interim, the Government should consider the following improvements: (i) allow commercialization of drawback rebates in the financial system, which may ease credit constraints for exporters. For those free of this constraint, it should make no difference whether to sell the rebates in the market or not, since it will be transacted at a discount equivalent to that created by the refund delay; (ii) recognize drawbacks to compensate for import duty costs to all exports, traditional or not; (iii) define the drawback clearly to prevent an implicit subsidy so that the relative price of importables and exportables is not affected and the relative price with respect to non-tradables is not raised; (iv) consider repealing the import duty rebate combined with exemption of exports from duties on imported inputs; and (v) extend the drawback to duties embodied on indirect inputs to fully compensate duties paid on imported inputs.

---

[4] Depending upon the technical input coefficients of a given export commodity, the average drawback may over- or under-compensate for the duties paid, thereby subsidizing or adding to costs, as the case may be.

[5] One could consider the exemption of local input producers from duties on their input requirements to give protection to these producers. The measure, however, does not fully offset the lack of protection from imported inputs on their portion of their sales, if any, to exporters of the final product. Hence an export drawback cum duty exemption on inputs utilized by local input producers would not in this case eliminate the discrimination against domestically produced inputs.

Facilitating technology diffusion and quality control

Globalization greatly increases the necessity to accelerate access to technology and upgrade related skills. Survey responses to questions on technology, production and business services illustrate the difficulties some firms face in reaching international technical standards. For a country like El Salvador it is hard to expect the development of indigenous technologies. In addition, private sector-driven initiatives are better suited to provide support services in the area of technology and production. The Government's role is to remove constraints and facilitate private sector efforts to gain access to technology and to enhance its capability of adapting to these new technologies by: (i) adopting and maintaining a liberal trade and investment regime; (ii) ensuring supportive human and physical infrastructure; and (iii) supporting private sector initiatives.

Supporting greater access to foreign technologies through trade and licensing agreements and foreign direct investment. The opening of the economy to trade and foreign investment is the most expedient route to the introduction of new technologies. For this to be possible, an adequate regime of intellectual property rights protection, hospitable to the inflow of foreign technology is needed. The signing of the property right agreement with the US is a step in that direction.

Ensuring supportive human and physical infrastructure. The most important constraints relate to human resource development, including the lack of basic vocational skills, the inability to diffuse and adapt to new technologies, and lack of attention to product quality. The focus should be on improving the quality of the human capital, but the Government can also facilitate innovation by supporting the development of telecommunications and information technology networks.

Encouraging development of private sector support services and initiatives. The private sector has been promoting efforts to modernize firms technologically and administratively but private- and public-sector provision of information about new production technologies as well as foreign markets is not fully satisfactory. The private and the public sector together should improve existing complementary support services to: (i) increase efforts to reach more exporters, particularly micro, small and medium firms, (ii) support firms in their efforts to comply with quality, technical and phytosanitary rules and to have greater access to technological innovations through support seminars and other dissemination activities; (iii) continue supporting promotional efforts to attract foreign direct investment. A review of issues and proposals to develop the public-private institutional framework supporting technology development, diffusion, and training may be found in the documentation of the World Bank Competitiveness Enhancement Technical Assistance Loan.

Strengthening trade negotiation capabilities

The Government should continue strengthening its trade negotiation capabilities to take full advantage of opportunities to increase access in new products and markets created by the successful conclusion of the Uruguay Round, the internationalization of services, and regional integration efforts. First, the Uruguay Round's achievements in improving market access and security are significant and are expected to accelerate globalization, but further unilateral and multilateral efforts will be necessary to take full advantage of opportunities. Second, the next stage of globalization is expected to be led by the internationalization of services, and countries will have to be actively involved in developments and negotiations relating to the General Agreement on Trade in Services. Third, in addition to attempting to revitalize the CACM, Central American countries, are trying to negotiate free trade agreements with non-CACM countries. El Salvador is currently holding free trade negotiations with Colombia and Venezuela, the Dominican Republic, Belize, and Mexico. El Salvador is also participating in the definition of the agenda for the implementation of the Free Trade Agreement of the Americas.

Improving government-business consultation

To accelerate private sector led-growth it is important to improve business-government interaction, by enhancing collaboration between the private and the public sector. In a number of countries, consultation between government and the private sector has enhanced decision making, strengthened government credibility, and generated greater consensus, transparency and follow-through on market oriented reforms. The establishment of FOMEX *(Comisión Nacional de Fomento de las Exportaciones)* to coordinate private and public sector efforts to encourage export development in February 1993 is a step forward. To strengthen this process, the Government should institutionalize one or more focused consultative committees of government and business representatives to discuss concrete steps to promote market-based reforms.

CHAPTER VI

STRENGTHENING THE FINANCIAL SECTOR

The dynamic recovery of the private sector owes much to the implementation of a credible stabilization and structural reform program since 1989. In particular, financial sector reforms - including the liberalization of interest rates, the restructuring and privatization of the banking system, and the creation of the capital market - have set the foundations for the development of a modern financial system. Nevertheless, more needs to be done to sustain and deepen these reforms. This chapter discusses constraints and policy options to improve access to credit; strengthen the banking system; and develop capital markets.

IMPROVING ACCESS TO CREDIT

Government efforts to ensure access to credit are focusing on: (i) creating space for the non-inflationary expansion of credit to the private sector (Chapter II); (ii) addressing collateral security issues; (iii) promoting use of new financing instruments; and (iv) facilitating access to credit by micro enterprises.

Addressing collateral security issues

Legal and regulatory constraints on using movable property as collateral limit access to credit. An efficient system for creating and enforcing security interests is key to improve access to credit and enable lenders, upon payment default, to foreclose and sell the security promptly and efficiently. In addition, such a system enables access to credit to those who do not own land or a title to land.

In El Salvador most credit to the private sector is supplied by commercial banks. Survey results showed that bank loans were the second principal source of financing (36 percent of total) after own capital to start an enterprise, and 60 percent of total anticipated financing for future investment. The most common collateral is real estate; followed by warehouse receipts and moveable assets, factoring, and discounting of financial paper. Many contemporary financing forms involve two steps. First, taking security interest in moveable and non-moveable property, largely possible through the Commercial Code. Second, lenders must be able to protect their security interests against claims of third parties by registering the security interest.[1] The collateral registration procedure is lengthy due to an unwarranted pre-registration procedure and does not provide creditors sufficient confidence in their security interests due to difficulties in perfecting and enforcing security interests.

Based on World Bank experience[2] the Government should consider:

⇨   **Creation of security interests:** change the legal framework to permit the creation of a wide variety of security interests in a wide variety of property;

⇨   **Perfection of security interests**: make public the records of registries, restructure the public registries, change the incentives by introducing competition among public registries or permit private registries to compete with public ones; and

⇨   **Enforcement of security interests**: change the law to permit private parties to contract for non-judicial enforcement of debt contracts.

---

[1]   Not all documentary security interests need to be filed at the registry in order to be secure, as possession of the original document is in some cases required to collect on pledged assets (Hansen ,1994). In fact, there are some receipts (e.g., warehouse), which are by nature secured by possession and cannot be claimed as collateral by a third party.

[2]   Summarized in FPD Note No.43 (World Bank, April 1995).

In addition, the Government should consider: (i) removing all pre-registration requirements when a potential borrower plans to grant a security interest in his land or movable property; and (ii) computerizing the registration of security interests.

Promoting the use of new financing instruments

Because of remaining issues related to establishing and securing property rights (Chapter IV) it is particularly important in the case of El Salvador to address the adequacy of the Commercial Code and related laws for contemporary financing contracts and commercial paper. Although the Code, which is based on the Mexican one, can accommodate innovations in certain areas, such as commercial financing, it is silent on a number of important areas (leasing, factoring, and warehousing) and grants judges discretion to look to commercial custom when adjudicating cases. In addition, other obstacles, such as lack of information networks and lack of explicit legal guidelines for advanced financing, suppress much financing activity, which is particularly important for microenterprises. The draft *Ley de Instituciones Auxiliares de Crédito* begins to address these issues by clarifying the operating parameters of financial institutions such as factoring houses, lease financing, and warehouse deposits, but a number of constraints still limit their use.

General constraints. El Salvador needs new financing vehicles. While most companies finance investments with internally generated funds, the ability of the private sector to become more competitive, and to seize new opportunities, will depend on the availability of medium- and long-term financing, as well as on the capacity to attract new investors via equity participation. Larger corporations have generally not encountered problems in financing working capital and, in some cases, qualifying for over one-year financing of fixed assets. But most companies that need to finance plant expansion, must rely on short-term revolving lines of credit with the consequent risk that the bank may cancel the line at any time. General constraints are related to the lack of explicit legal guidelines for advanced financing.

Leasing and factoring. Current issues relate to: title to and possession of leased goods; insurance and risk of loss; sales and subleasing of goods by lessee; priority of liens; and other rights of lessor and lessee. Leases are covered by basic contract provisions of the Commercial Code. Despite the lack of specific regulation, factoring and discounting of commercial paper are available through individuals and at least one company.

Liens on inventory. The Commercial Code allows liens on inventory, but the provisions are limited because: (i) liens on commercial inventory held in a warehouse are excluded. This type of liens has advantages over warehouse receipts in that the entrepreneur may freely trade the warehoused goods; and (ii) banks do not favor liens on inventory because recording at the Commercial Registry requires listing every item in the inventory in order to secure each of them. In addition, to secure floating liens on inventory, the security interest must be self-executing, which means creating a public document that is authorized by the court, notarized, etc. This is expensive and cumbersome.

Liens on commercial equipment. Lenders often take liens on equipment, usually as part of a larger collateral package, such as a mortgage. Decision-making regarding these liens rests with the Government as: (i) the Commercial Code regulates what property can be pledged as collateral, as well as time limitations on the loans themselves; and (ii) article 1158 allows only one lien to exist on any moveable good at one time, regardless of its amount. Although this may seem to protect lenders, it is not consistent with market principles and may unnecessarily tie up valuable collateral.

To expand use of advanced financing:

⇨ set guidelines on the use of new financing instruments in the *Ley de Instituciones Auxiliares de Crédito,* particularly for leasing, factoring, and discounting of commercial paper;

⇨ ensure uniform treatment of issues related to specific business financing instruments;

⇨ expand use of liens on inventory by: (i) including in the Commercial Code provisions for liens on commercial inventory held in a warehouse; (ii) allowing a more general description of the inventory to satisfy security registration; and (iii) streamlining the procedure to secure floating liens on inventory; and

⇨ in the area of liens on commercial equipment, shift economic decision-making and risk-taking from the Government to the private sector by: (i) liberalizing articles 1144 and 1148-55 of the Commercial Code to shift risk assessment and term negotiation to private actors; and (ii) removing unwarranted provision in Article 1158 permitting only one lien on moveable assets.

Lending to microenterprises: policy options and lessons from experience

To improve access to financing by microenterprises, the Government should try new approaches, taking into consideration the following lessons:[3]

⇨ **Strategy**: the best programs - in terms of impact and financial viability - are a small number of large micro-credit operations which reach a significant number of enterprises primarily with financial services and limited technical assistance, typically in loan application and follow-up. Successful examples include: the Grameen Bank of Bangladesh, Indonesia's BRI/Kupedes program, Banco Solidario in Bolivia, ADEMI in the Dominican Republic, and the Kenya Rural Enterprise Program;

⇨ **Packaging**: experience shows that: (i) building viable micro-credit systems takes several years and (ii) that financial services need to be provided in a businesslike way if programs are to be sustainable; micro enterprise borrowers should pass merit tests by demonstrating their qualifications to operate small enterprises and to undertake the responsibility of a loan;

⇨ **Delivery**: strengthening the capacity of intermediaries, usually NGOs, to manage programs and appraise loans is critical; and

⇨ **Terms and conditions**: three features have been key: (i) price services based on costs; (ii) focus on providing working capital; and (iii) include savings mobilization.

STRENGTHENING THE BANKING SYSTEM

The banking system has been restructured and privatized, but the Government now needs to further liberalize and strengthen the banking system to enhance its capacity to absorb large changes in liquidity and ensure the existence of a strong and independent superintendency. The authorities should continue focusing on upgrading the regulatory and prudential framework by: (i) increasing competition; (ii) lowering illiquidity risks; (iii) strengthening supervision; and (iv) establishing deposit insurance.

Increasing competition

Current regulations impose two types of limitations on ownership based on nationality and on a 5 percent rule for privatized institutions. These limitations should be reconsidered. In addition, the Central Bank should ensure the availability of more accurate interest rate information to enhance transparency.

---

[3] Summarized in FPD Note No.23 (World Bank , September 1994).

Eliminating ownership limits. Total assets of the banking system represent about 50 percent of GDP. Most of these institutions were privatized beginning in 1991, after being restructured and recapitalized. Seven banks initiated operations between 1994 and early 1995, stimulated by high returns on capital (in the order of 20 percent). The two largest banks control almost 50 percent of the market and there are no foreign banks. Legislation requires that only Salvadoran nationals (or Central American nationals if reciprocity exists) can be majority stockholders in banks or finance companies incorporated in El Salvador. This forces foreign banks to either become minority partners or create a new institution, such as a branch office. The Government is currently preparing draft legislation to address this limitation to foster the participation of foreign banks in the financial system, both through the incorporation of new institutions or through the purchase of existing banks. It should also consider the relaxation of the 5 percent rule (per individual, corporation, affiliated groups or related individuals) for privatized institutions, since it does not apply to new banks or finance companies. Banks subject to the 5 percent ownership rule could be at a disadvantage in raising new capital compared to the unrestricted banks which could raise capital from just one or several large stockholders.

Ensuring accurate interest rate information. To enhance transparency in the credit market, the Central Bank or the Superintendency of the Financial System (SSF) should calculate and publish - at least weekly - an average adjusted costs of funds rate. Currently each institution calculates and publishes its own arbitrary reference rate. The proposed change would ensure that interest rate differentials among institutions reflect only a spread over a common reference rate.

Lowering illiquidity risks

The Central Bank should develop regulations to decrease existing illiquidity risks. Illiquidity risks result from the increase in the volume of funds being intermediated by the financial system without well developed bank supervision. Given the preference for short-term deposits, banks may increase their risk exposure by mismatching the maturities of loans (long-term) and deposits (short-term). The structure of deposits highlights the continued preference for short-term instruments: 13 percent of total deposits are sight deposits, 32 percent are savings deposits, and 55 percent time deposits. Since savings account are 100 percent liquid, this deposit structure increases illiquidity risks because approximately 45 percent of total deposits are completely liquid. The Government should consider establishing minimum liquidity requirements or enacting, as in the case of Panama, regulations requiring banks to maintain open foreign credit lines equivalent to 10 percent of their assets.

Strengthening supervision of the banking system

While much progress has been achieved in training of bank examiners, preparation of procedures manuals, and implementing risk asset classification standards, additional work is needed to strengthen SSF's preventive supervision capabilities. Action to strengthen SSF was taken in December 1990, with the passage of a new Organic Law of the Financial System Superintendency which empowers SSF to act as primary supervisor of the financial system. To perform its new responsibilities, SSF was reorganized around four divisions: (i) banks and finance companies; (ii) insurance and pension funds; (iii) securities exchange; and (iv) administration and finance. However, specific SSF responsibilities in regulating the capital markets and the insurance and pension industries need to be defined by additional legislation.

Implementing a rating system. Although there are a limited number of banks, the rating of banks would strengthen SFF prudential supervision. At the same time, a quantitative rating index would give a financial intermediary a more precise gauge of its performance, and could also be used in determining at what point the regulators could begin to take preventive action with respect to a weakening institution. An often used methodology that could be utilized in evaluating financial intermediaries is the CAMEL rating system which reviews capital adequacy, asset quality, management capabilities, earnings performance, and liquidity.

Strengthening information and accounting standards. Since transparency of information is crucial for investors to properly evaluate risks of financial institutions, the SFF has been publishing extensive information on bank financial statements and the classification of risk assets by individual institution. This already excellent source of information could be enhanced with selected financial ratios including the capital ratios based on the regulatory definition of capital and risk assets.

Accelerating training and development. The need for ongoing training and development of supervision cannot be over-emphasized. The integrity of the financial system rests on the capabilities of its regulatory agencies. This analysis does not necessarily conclude that more regulations are needed, but rather that stronger enforcement of existing rules should be emphasized.

Establishing a deposit insurance fund

The authorities should accelerate efforts to implement a well functioning deposit insurance fund. Deposit protection has three positive effects: (i) it offers the Government and the taxpayers some protection against contagious bank runs; (ii) it protects small depositors which do not have the information to evaluate the financial condition of individual banks; and (iii) may foster higher savings and promote financial intermediation.

The establishment of deposit insurance is contemplated in the Banking Law but is not functioning yet. Deposit insurance systems are complex to design and implement and the IMF is providing technical assistance in this process. In general, the authorities should consider:[4]

⇨ **Amount of protection:** protection should be by depositor and limited (i.e., small depositor-oriented) to a relatively small amount;
⇨ **Proper funding**: it is difficult to predict the losses that the deposit insurer will have to absorb over the years and at the same time it is extremely dangerous for the insurer to become illiquid. The best way to ensure proper funding is by: (i) providing the insurer with adequate initial capital to give the insurer credibility; (ii) having insured banks make reasonable periodic premium payments into the fund; and (iii) giving the insurer legal authority to borrow or receive equity injections from the Government to honor its obligation to protect depositors; and
⇨ **Flexibility**: the deposit insurer should be given maximum flexibility in resolving failing bank situations, so long as the method employed is consistent with the stated objectives of the fund.

DEVELOPING CAPITAL MARKETS

Financial markets complement banking institutions in mobilizing and delivering investment resources, particularly in the case of longer-term, larger-scale, and higher risk investments. The public sector can play an important role in helping build local financial markets by: (i) issuing public securities thus acting as a catalyst; (ii) enforcing standards of fairness in trading and broad disclosure of information; (iii) strengthening prudential regulation; and (iv) developing enabling legislation for the reform and more active involvement of financial intermediaries.

---

[4] FPD Note No.12 (World Bank, June 1994).

Catalyzing the supply of securities

One of the main constraints behind the development of the securities market in El Salvador is the dearth of potential private sector issuers. Factors limiting private sector participation include: (i) private companies are not very large and those that could access the public market, have relied on traditional sources of finance, such as bank loans, and private placements with insurance companies; and (ii) most businesses are closely held family enterprises; which generally do not view a pubic issue favorably because of disclosure requirements and, in the case of share issues, the possibility of management interference or even loss of management control.

As the private sector develops, companies will probably begin issuing shares through the stock market but the "cultural change" of opening up companies to the public will take time. In the interim, the public sector can play an important role in building up the securities market by establishing benchmarks as an active security issuer and to help provide liquidity to the markets. It should actively manage the issuance of its own debt securities and the equity in state-owned enterprises to be privatized. These public issues play an important role in catalyzing private sector development by offering simple structural design, pricing benchmarks, and liquidity.

In addition, the Government should enhance collaborative efforts within CACM to allow regional trading of securities. Initial steps have been taken to consider alternative market schemes and the establishment of a common regulatory environment. While full integration within a regional capital market is still far off, the outlook is encouraging. Through the formation of a regional securities exchange, CACM countries could overcome scale constraints faced by each market.

Ensuring reliable and timely disclosure of information

Current issues include: (i) insufficient disclosure of financial information; tightly-held corporations have little interest in revealing the financial condition of their businesses or diluting ownership. When these companies approach the capital market, they resist public disclosure. This is the case of the prospectuses that have been issued for all public offerings of investment certificates. Financial statements are highly condensed with little information other than a few financial ratios. It is imperative to develop greater transparency of information in the securities market to protect investors from undue risk, and to improve market access to profitable but not well known companies; (ii) public accounting firms do not follow generally accepted industry standards, which compromises the reliability of audited financial statements to assess the financial position of borrowers. Lending is therefore done primarily on the basis of collateral; and (iii) periodic information on current market trends is lacking.

To ensure reliable and timely disclosure of information the Government should: (i) support the development of reliable risk rating agencies; (ii) encourage public accounting firms to establish a self-regulatory body which adopts and enforces generally accepted accounting principles; and (iii) ensure availability of periodic information on transactions in the exchange, including summary statistics on prices, volumes and yields. Financial information on listed companies should be compiled by industry in order to provide useful indicators on sectoral trends and performance.

Strengthening supervision

While substantial progress has been achieved in bank supervision, supervision of the securities exchange as well as insurance and pensions needs strong institutional development within SSF. The lack of adequate supervision in these areas is attributed to: (i) the emphasis given so far, and rightly so, to the development of banking supervision; (ii) the absence of comprehensive legislation regarding capital markets, insurance, and pensions that would provide SSF a clear mandate; and (iii) lack of resources to develop an effective supervisory role. Technical assistance from IDB will strengthen supervision of the securities exchange; substantial resources will be needed to improve staffing, hardware and software. In addition, the development of capital markets should be monitored closely by SSF in terms of the impact on the banking system. The issuance of investment certificates directly by corporate borrowers will intensify competition with banks who must retain their good corporate customers by offering better terms than what they can receive in the securities market. Since banks are allowed to own brokerage houses, financial institutions are planning to expand into this area.

Facilitating the development of financial intermediaries

The development of institutional investors, such as insurance companies and pension funds, and investment companies is essential to deepen capital markets. The priority is to draft and enact enabling legislation for institutional investors while overhauling the contractual savings system.

Insurance companies. The liberalization of the insurance industry is an indispensable step to promote new products, while generating a solid base of long-term funds that could be invested in private sector projects. The insurance industry has developed without an effective legal and regulatory framework. The Government is discussing new legislation to govern the insurance and pension industries. The overriding objective should be to establish a level playing field for all financial intermediaries within an effective regulatory environment. The insurance industry has grown through sales of property and casualty products and all but two companies offer life, property and casualty coverage. The lack of a sufficient array of investment instruments in the market has limited insurance company investments to bank deposits, government securities, and certain private placements. These companies are eager to see the securities market develop to diversify their investments, and have recently started to offer new products such as universal life which competes with other savings instruments.

The Government should focus on the drafting and enactment of new insurance legislation, to: (i) enhance supervision and greater flexibility in market development; (ii) probably separate life and non-life insurance business considering that risks are quite distinct, although they could operate under a single holding company; (iii) supplement minimum capital requirements with a system of dynamic solvency margins. The margins should be designed to protect policy holders as they automatically supplement shareholder equity and are set aside in a guarantee fund. Minimum capital standards should be increased, and companies that fail to meet these requirements should be encouraged to merge with larger firms; and (iv) improve the supervisory role of SSF. This will require raising the standards and effectiveness of off-site supervision and on-site inspections of insurance companies. One option would be to split the Superintendency division for insurance companies and pension funds into two.

Social security reform and pension funds. The Government is undertaking a fundamental reform of the social security system to move toward fully funded defined contribution accounts The immediate priority for the social security and pension fund system is financial restructuring and recapitalization. The Salvadoran Social Security Institute (ISSS) and the National Civil Servants' Retirement Fund (INPEP) are struggling with rising payouts relative to contributions. Both systems work on a pay-as-you-go basis. Key issues include the following:

⇨ *Solvency problems:* Barring prompt action, both institutions are likely to face solvency problems. Privatization of the pension industry is being studied but its restructuring is likely to require sizable transfers from the Government in order to re-capitalize the two funds (ISSS and INPEP);

⇨ *Inappropriate structure:* The current structure could be characterized as three separate entities involved in the same activities, but each using different pricing mechanisms, and offering a mixture of services not directly related to the underlying activity of retirement benefits. The pension system only covers about 18 percent of the economically active population with the vast majority in urban areas. The rest of the population must rely on their own resources, and any other limited Government benefits they can access;

⇨ *Commingling of funds:* The commingling of health care and pension funds seriously undermines the financial integrity of the pension component. The health care portion of ISSS has experienced deficits which were covered with pension fund reserves. ISSS, the country's largest pension fund, receives direct contributions from the Government, as well as compulsory salary deductions from employees and payments by employers. In addition to pension coverage, the ISSS provides basic health care benefits to both public and private sector contributors but it does not provide unemployment insurance. Both the pension and the health care programs are combined within ISSS's global fund, even though they are strictly separate operations. The separation of the pension and health care funds should be considered; and

⇨ *Restrictive investment strategies:* Investment strategies are constrained by rigid rules, and generate low returns. Several factors account for this, among them, a lack of management expertise, an excessive number of low-paid, under-qualified staff, and a high degree of evasion and avoidance by employers. For example, about 80 percent of ISSS investments are in time deposits, the rest mostly in mortgage certificates and Government bonds. Greater flexibility in investment policy, within a manageable risk profile, could significantly enhance earnings.

The Government is undertaking a fundamental reform of the contractual savings system to move from a pay-as-you-go defined benefit system to fully funded defined contribution accounts, along the Chilean approach.[5] The immediate priority is a financial restructuring and recapitalization by the Government, followed by implementation of adequate policies and procedures regarding pricing of coverage and investment of accumulated reserves.

Mutual funds and leasing companies. The establishment of mutual funds and leasing companies could become an important source of institutional demand for securities. No mutual funds exist in El Salvador, and their introduction would require additional legislation to permit the formation of investment companies. The appeal of the mutual fund as an investment vehicle is the ability to pool many small investors, while it could invest in certain private placements of securities. Through this arrangement, a small investor could participate in potential profits from a company that goes public, while the company pursues the less restrictive alternative of a private placement. Investment advisers and investment companies are still not allowed to operate, but the development of mutual funds hinges on the availability of investment management firms to manage customer portfolios.

Leasing companies are another type of financial intermediary which can act as a catalyst to the development of the medium-term funds market. Leasing companies could become an option for small- to mid-sized companies that do not have access to capital markets. The advantage of a leasing company is that the lender retains title to the goods, while the borrower has the tax advantage of full deduction of lease payments. Leasing companies issue medium-term notes in the market to finance the acquisition of machinery and equipment, they then offer leases to their customers on terms which usually coincide with the economic life of the asset. Typically, a lease contract would include an option to purchase the fixed assets, at some predetermined residual price, at the end of the lease.

The Government should consider enacting legislation to allow the establishment of mutual funds and leasing companies. In particular, consideration should be given to the promotion of domestic mutual funds, that could be established initially to invest in those securities available in the market, such as

---

[5]   Chile instituted a Government-regulated but privately-run mandatory savings system supplemented by a pay-as-you-go public plan that guarantees a minimum benefit to workers with low incomes or interrupted employment careers who are not able to save enough for adequate pensions.

Government securities and investment certificates, and eventually expand their portfolio to incorporate equities. All properly regulated financial intermediaries, such as commercial banks and finance companies, should be allowed to offer their own mutual funds through an affiliate investment company. The establishment of investment companies should also be promoted, which could offer money market mutual funds by investing in existing bank CDs and investment certificates. The minimum purchase amount for an investment certificate is about 10,000 colones (about US$1,100) which leaves out a large percentage of savers. Whereas a mutual fund could offer the same investment opportunity at a much lower minimum amount.

ANNEX

Constraints to Private Enterprises:
A Summary of Survey Results[1]

Introduction. El Salvador's economy is in a dynamic period of adjustment and growth. Stabilization and liberalization have already enhanced opportunities for private enterprise and there seems to be a broad social commitment to peace and growth. Yet a large agenda for reform and institutional strengthening remains and its priorities must in part be guided by the needs of private entrepreneurs starting, operating and expanding their firms.

It is now well-recognized that private sector development (PSD) will be critical to overall economic prosperity and increased standards of living. Thus it is essential to identify those factors that limit this development. One key instrument that has proven effective is the enterprise survey, which elicits the judgments of entrepreneurs and senior managers on the severity of constraints to PSD.

Sample Characteristics. This annex describes the results of a survey of 210 firms designed by the World Bank and refined and implemented by FUSADES (Fundacion Salvadoreña para el Desarrollo Economico y Social). Figure 1 describes the size and sectoral composition of the stratified sample. The main sample consisted of 177 large, medium and small enterprises, while a supplementary, shorter questionnaire was administered to a sample of 33 microenterprises. Geographically, the survey was carried out in three urban areas: San Salvador (58% of firms sampled), Santa Ana (22%), and San Miguel (20%). The sample was a combination of a panel, which comprised part of an ongoing FUSADES study of the business climate, and firms randomly selected within strata. Larger and industrial firms are over-represented in the sample.

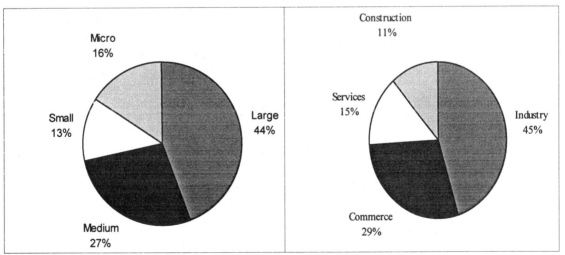

Figure 1: Sample Characteristics

Enterprises in the sample are generally fairly old -- averaging over 23 years in operation. While age is somewhat correlated with size, even micro-enterprises averaged over 14 years old.

---

[1] All tables and figures in this annex are based on the results of the World Bank/FUSADES private enterprise survey.

This suggests that much of the economic dynamism is coming from the growth of existing firms rather than from new firms. It may also draw attention to the possibility of entry barriers.[2] Some 94% of firms in the sample are registered (including 74% of microenterprises), so the sample may have favored somewhat formal and more established firms.

Table 1: *Characteristics of El Salvador Sample*

Size	Small	Medium	Large
Ave. No. Employees	16	120	590
Ave. Annual Sales (millions of Colones)	2.9	43.4	143.3

The survey gathered data on firm procurement, sales and investment. One striking pattern is the "trade deficit" and inward orientation: firms purchase 49% of their inputs from abroad, yet export only 12% of their production. For example, over 21% of inputs are purchased from El Salvador's principal trading partner, the United States, yet only 4.5% of products and services are sold there. Industrial and commercial firms import the most (47.9% and 35%), but commercial firms export little (2%) while industrial firms export some 22% of their production. This inward orientation may help to explain why, in a time of recovery, many firms report having excess capacity. Enterprises reported operating at 73% of installed capacity, on average. Industrial sector firms, operating at 75%, did somewhat better than average, and both large and microenterprises were closer to capacity than small and medium ones. When asked why they don't produce more, 27% of firms explained that internal demand was insufficient and 13% said there was too much competition -- signs of too many firms competing in a small domestic market.

Table 2A: *Sources of inputs for Salvadoran Firms*

PERCENT	TOTAL	SECTOR				SIZE		
	%	**Industry**	**Commerce**	**Services**	**Construction**	**Large**	**Medium**	**Small**
Produced in El Salvador	50.8	47.9	35.0	60.2	81.8	47.1	53.9	56.9
Imported from Ctrl. America and Mexico	13.1	14.9	15.3	5.9	8.1	14.3	10.5	12.6
Imported from U.S.	21.2	23.4	22.6	22.6	9.8	23.6	21.5	12.6
Imported from Rest of World	15.1	13.7	27.1	11.3	0.3	15.0	14.1	17.2

Table 2B: *Destination of Sales for Salvadoran Firms*

PERCENT	TOTAL	SECTOR				SIZE		
	%	**Industry**	**Commerce**	**Services**	**Construction**	**Large**	**Medium**	**Small**
Sold to Domestic Market	87.9	77.8	97.7	92.5	100.0	83.2	92.1	95.2
Exported to Central America and Mexico	5.9	11.5	1.3	1.4	0.0	8.6	3.9	1.5
Exported to U.S.	4.5	7.7	0.7	4.8	0.0	6.4	2.4	2.2
Exported to Rest of World	1.7	3.0	0.4	1.3	0.0	1.8	1.7	1.1

---

[2] It could potentially reflect a sampling bias, if the list from which the survey was drawn includes only older firms. However, the list used was the most complete available and the newest firms in the sample were only 1 year old.

Nearly 40% of enterprises make some sales to the Government or public enterprises, accounting for an average of 21% of sales for the entire sample. Sales to the Government sharply increase with firm size, with 56% of large firms having government sales versus only 6% of microenterprises. By sector, fully half of construction firms sell to the government or public enterprises, which accounts for 46% of their sales. By location, firms in San Salvador are far more likely to have public business with half making public sector sales. Firms making sales to the government identified two moderate problems: excessive paperwork and bureaucracy, and late payment. Construction firms also complained of limited competency of public officials supervising their contracts.

General Constraints. Firms were asked in the survey to rank a number of constraints to their operation and growth on a scale from 1 to 5, where a one indicated the constraint imposed "no obstacle", a 3 indicated a "moderate obstacle", and a 5 indicated a "very severe" obstacle. It was quite striking that few firms ranked any constraints a 4 or 5, and average scores were generally low compared to other similar country studies. Figure 3 demonstrates the low average ranking of constraints in El Salvador compared to other countries where similar surveys have been conducted. While cultural factors may partially explain these low scores, much can be explained by the relative improvement of the business environment resulting from the end of the civil war and the reform policies already in place. Compared to how bad things were, few constraints appear "very severe" now. Nonetheless, most firms identified some constraint as major or very severe: 66% of the main sample and 79% of the microenterprise sample identified at least one constraint as at least "major". Figure 2 illustrates the rankings of constraints provided by the survey responses.

While new-found stability helps explain the overall low ranking of constraints, the survey shows that instability of prices and government remain the dominant concerns of enterprises, even in the post-civil war era. The desire for stability and security in the business climate is reinforced by the next constraints: problems of security -- mostly related to increasing "common delinquency": theft and other crimes -- policy instability and the exchange rate. Close behind are concerns about finance, human resources and the level of taxes. While these rankings accurately reflect the firms' relative assessment of these constraints, it should be noted that when entrepreneurs were asked at the beginning of the survey what were their leading problems (and no specific categories of constraints were offered), the two most commonly cited constraints were the lack of competent workers and problems of finance.

Smaller firms are especially concerned with financial constraints (Figure 3). Micro firms felt particularly concerned with the functioning of the judicial system and with problems of acquiring inputs (possibly tied to limited working capital and an inability to import directly). Construction firms, currently booming by most accounts, identified themselves as more constrained than firms in other sectors in a number of areas, led by inflation, political and policy uncertainty, finance, and the exchange rate (Figure 4). Driven by the building boom, some of these firms appear to be pushing at the boundaries of their production frontiers, confronting limitations in policies, institutions and markets. Although taxes and regulations did not rank as major constraints, firms were quite disturbed by informal competition, suggesting significant cost advantages to those who evaded these constraints (see below).

FIGURE 2

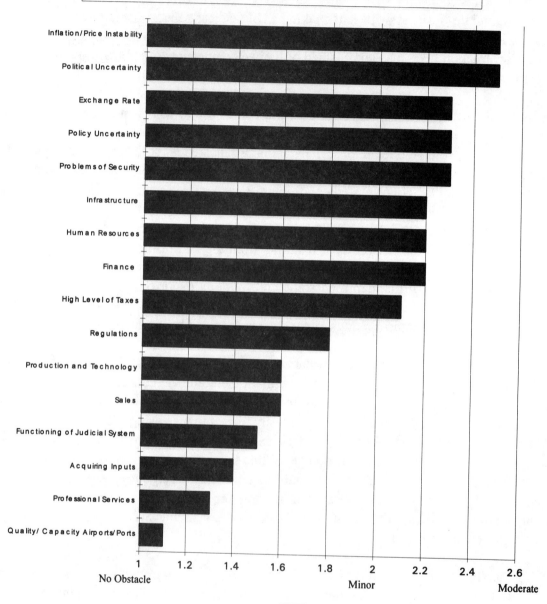

Obstacles to Salvadoran Enterprise Operation and Growth

Severity of Constraint

Figure 3. Constraints to Salvadoran Enterprises by Size

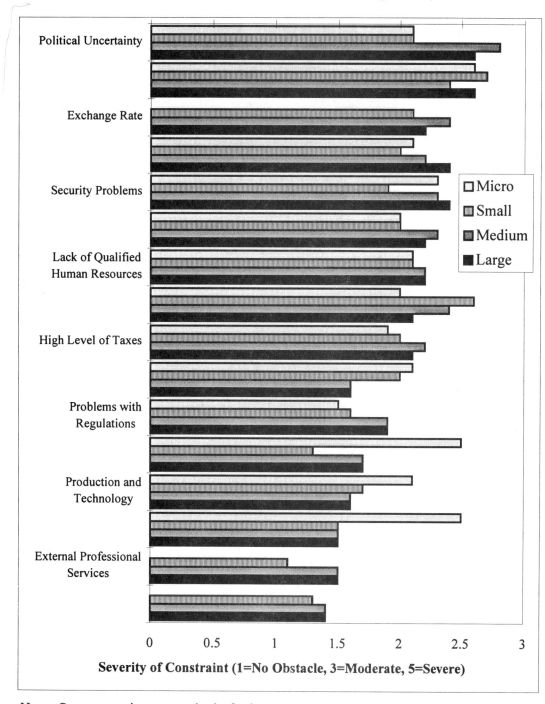

Note: Some questions not asked of microenterprises.

Figure 4. Constraints to Salvadoran Enterprises by Sector

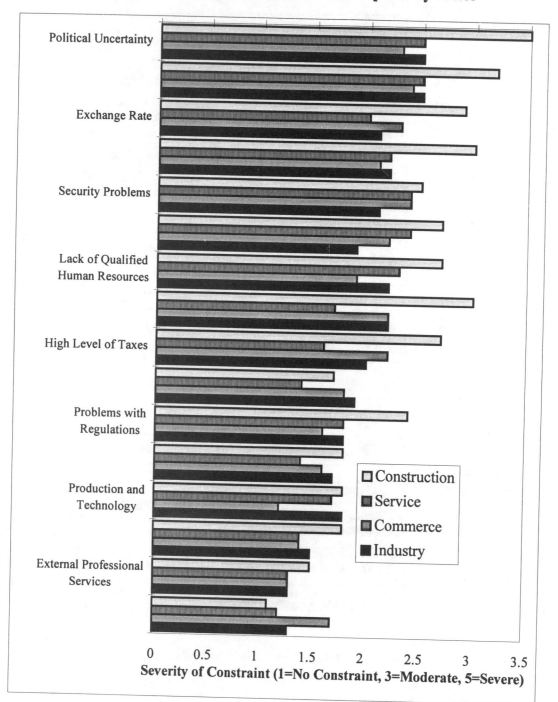

Regulation. Regulations were not in general regarded as very constraining, and constraint rankings were extremely low by international standards (table 4). Nonetheless, the prevalence of informal competition and direct data from firms about compliance costs suggests that regulatory requirements impose significant costs on firms. It is important to note that 72% of firms in the main sample and 85% of microenterprises found no area of regulation more than moderately constraining. In their responses, only construction firms found any regulatory constraint more than minor: they identified obtaining permits and the number of permits and licenses required as excessive, rating it a moderate constraint. Although firms found no major constraints among regulations, qualitative responses suggest they found an annoying excess of minor obstacles: in obtaining licensees and the number of permits and licenses required; and in tax regulations. Microenterprises found few difficulties among regulations, although a small minority found tax procedures and, especially the value added tax, difficult.

Despite regulation's low ranking, its costs are significant. Firms reported that their senior managers or owners spend on average over 7% of their time on activities required by government. For construction firms, this is substantially higher -- almost 12% of senior management time is spent working with permits, taxes, labor regulations and customs. A further 5% of employee time is required to comply with regulations. Furthermore, although firms did not single out customs or ports, it takes them an average of 15 days from the time goods arrive in customs to the time they can be claimed.

Firms offered surprisingly strong responses about the problem of informal competition, providing further evidence of the costs of regulation and the advantages realized by to those who avoid it. 59% of firms experienced problems with informal or illegal competition. It was most common in commerce, where some 74% of firms identified the problem. The four topmost concerns were: competitors evading the value-added and other taxes, firms selling below costs, firms avoiding customs and trade regulations, and firms avoiding labor regulations and taxes. Note that three of the four topmost concerns in this regard involve avoidance of taxes and regulations.

Formal entry appears neither especially difficult nor expensive. Some 67% of enterprises indicated that they had encountered no difficult steps in registering. Formalizing an enterprise (including official fees and costs of facilitation) cost an average of 3,800 colones, but for some firms cost as little as 500, and for one industrial enterprise cost as much as 15,000. Industrial and construction firms generally paid more to register. According to FUSADES analysis, of firms that registered in the last three years, the average cost of registration (2015 colones) amounted to only 1.83% of annual sales. However, for firms that registered in the last 10 years, registration appears to have been time consuming. Omitting a few outliers -- it took firms an average of 15 weeks to become formal.

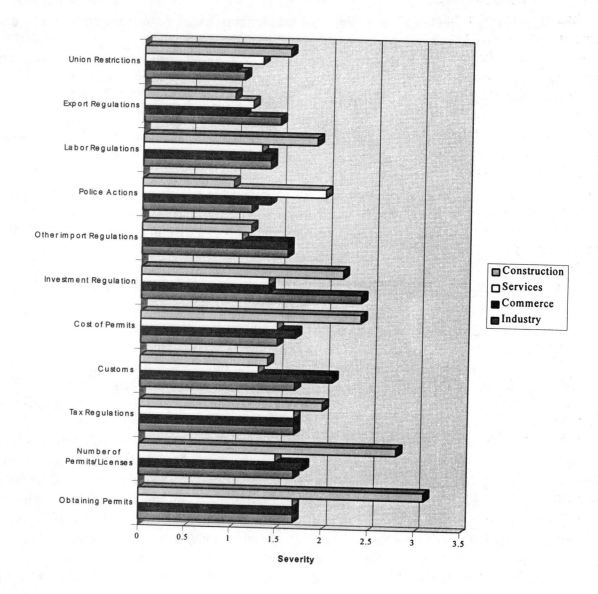

Regulatory Constraints to Salvadoran Enterprises

Legend:
- Construction
- Services
- Commerce
- Industry

Figure 5

Labor regulations and union activity were not constraints for most firms sampled, and were ranked the lowest among Latin American countries surveyed to date (Figure 6). Some 14% of enterprises had unionized workers, concentrated primarily among construction firms and roughly correlated with size. However, only 6% had experienced a strike in the last five years. Among those firms, the average strike duration was 13 days and the cost was 1.5 million colones (an average influenced heavily by large and construction firms). Firing appears to be easy, and some 64% of enterprises reported having dismissed a worker in the last year for any reason. On average, the process took about 3 days, depending on the enterprise's own policies. More important in labor constraints was the availability of capable workers -- a constraint that came in first in the open-ended question on constraints to firms. Among supply constraints, finding skilled workers ranked slightly ahead of problems finding technicians and managers, but all were considered to be minor constraints.

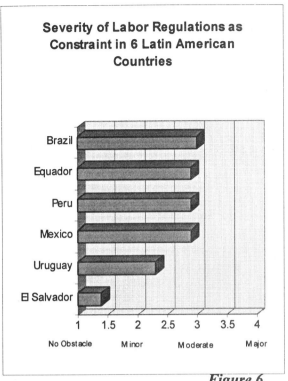

Figure 6

Infrastructure. Infrastructure imposed only minor to moderate constraints on most firms. It is nonetheless worth noting that 40% of firms, including 58% of construction sector firms, said that problems of transportation and communication created difficulties in fulfilling agreements for the timely delivery of their products. The three leading constraints were the state of roads, problems with telecommunications, and voltage fluctuations. Roads are especially limiting to those firms that export the most -- larger and industrial firms. Construction firms were most frustrated with the state of telecommunications, ranking it their leading infrastructural constraint. Finally, voltage fluctuations imposed a moderate constraint on firms, more so on large and medium firms. Geographically, firms in San Miguel were especially bothered by infrastructural limitations, including roads, telecom and electricity, perhaps a residual of the physical damage caused by the civil war. Almost all firms had telephones, with the exception of 27% of the microenterprise subsample (disproportionately concentrated in San Miguel). Although telephone service ranked low as a constraint, over half of respondents were dissatisfied with the number of lines they had. The overwhelming reason cited for not having more telephones was that ANTEL had no additional lines to give them. The waiting time for a new line was estimated at 21 weeks in San Salvador, 18 weeks in Santa Ana, and 70 weeks in San Miguel. Firms in San Miguel were also worse off in terms of the number of weeks per year their telephones were out of service (an average of 2.9) and the number of times they had to dial to complete a local (5.8) or international (3.5) call. Perhaps one reason telephones were not more severe constraints is that 45% of firms owned radios to communicate, led by 56% of firms in San Salvador. Access to land did not seem to be a severe constraining: 67% of respondents owned all or part of the land where their firm was located (ownership was correlated with size), and all but 0.5% of firms owned or leased their property.

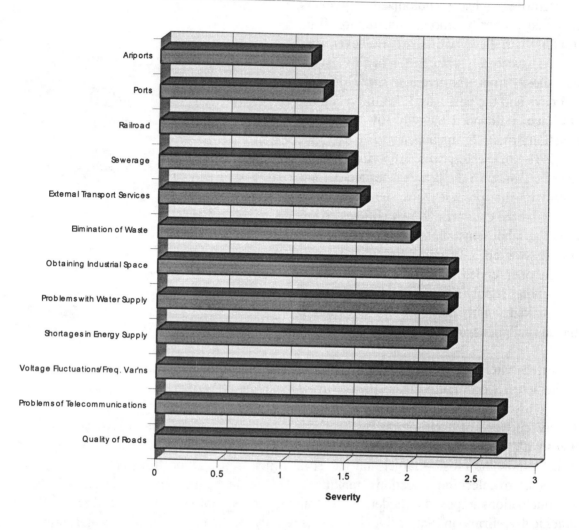

Figure 7

Finance. In the area of finance, firms were most concerned with high interest rates (table 5). Firms in construction especially noticed this moderate constraint (in part due to their customer's cost of mortgages). Collateral imposed a minor constraint on firms but, again, was more severe for those in construction. Small firms were more constrained than medium and large firms by collateral requirements, while medium-sized firms found interest rates most limiting. To start an enterprise, the principal source of financing is own capital (just over half), followed by bank loans - - 36% of total. Small and micro firms rely more heavily on their own funds than do medium and large firms. One finding that violated our expectations was a low reliance on friends and family overseas. We had expected to find substantial reliance on relatives working overseas and lending capital, but this was not identified as important. For some service firms and microenterprises, friends and family in El Salvador provided more than 10% of funds, but friends and family outside of El Salvador were not important. For future investment, commercial banks (60%) and own funds dominated.

Table 3. Financial Constraints to Salvadoran Firms

Average Constraint Scores (1-5)	SECTOR				SIZE			
	Industry	Commerce	Services	Construction	Large	Medium	Small	Micro
Guarantees/Sec'ty Required	2.3	2.3	2.0	2.7	2.1	2.5	2.7	2.3
Documentation Required	1.7	1.9	1.7	1.7	1.5	1.9	2.0	2.0
Interest Rates	2.6	2.7	2.3	2.9	2.6	2.8	2.5	2.5
Reqm't of Deposit/ Track Record	1.8	1.8	1.7	1.9	1.4	1.7	1.8	2.0
Don't have right Connections	1.6	1.7	1.5	1.7	1.4	1.7	1.8	2.0

Table reflects average constraint scores where a 1 means "no obstacle", a 2 a "minor obstacle" and a 3 a "moderate obstacle".

One important constraint to business transactions evidenced by survey responses relates to credit information and collection. Firms indicated through several responses that they have a difficult time determining the reliability of customers and a tough time with repayment. First, the results show that fewer than half (46.2%) of firms extend credit to new customers who are not personal acquaintances. This is much lower than several other Latin American countries.

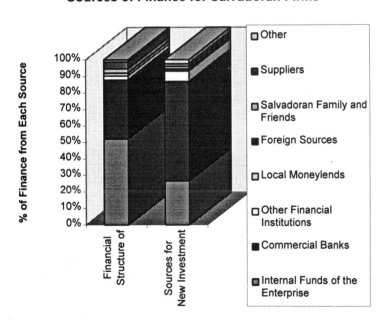

Sources of Finance for Salvadoran Firms

Figure 8

When they do offer such credit, they must principally rely on directly checking references, although some 30% sometimes make use of a credit agency. Credit checking through an agency is much more common among large and medium firms (small firms don't do it) and in San Salvador, where half of firms sometimes use this means. Firms estimate that some 27% (median value of 20%) of clients pay their debts late, and 5% allow their debts to become delinquent (median value of 2%). When clients don't pay, over 30% of cases are simply written off. About 61% are resolved through a negotiated partial payment.

However, a surprisingly high 19% end up in court. In fact, the average firm identified nearly 6 cases in the last two year that it had taken to court. Large firms were most likely to pursue this formal means and commerce firms far more active in resolution of debts than other firms, including through the courts.

Security Concerns. Problems of security or "common delinquency" were the fifth leading obstacle cited by firms in the open-ended question. Some 44% of firms said they had taken special measures to protect their enterprise, led by 61% of large enterprises. (Microenterprises were not asked this question). Of those taking such measures, 66% employed guards, 27% took out insurance, 14% installed grills or bars, and 13% built special walls. Among those firms taking such measures, the average monthly expenditure was 29,000 colones, a figure heavily influenced by large firms, which averaged a monthly expenditure of 44,000 colones. Only one third of small firms took special security precautions, and those that did spent an average of 3,600 colones per month. Enterprises estimated that, in nominal terms, their expenditures on security had increased 85% over the last five years, led by an increase of almost 300% for small enterprises.

Business Services. Finally, lack of business or professional services were of little concern to the firms surveyed. However, about 48% of firms acknowledged receiving some complaints about the quality of their product or service and 5% said they had regular complaints. Businesses reported that their most important sources of technical production information were suppliers and clients.

Microenterprises. As noted at the beginning, microenterprises were included in a special supplementary sample and administered a shorter questionnaire. The microenterprises in the sample were, to a surprising extent, formal enterprises and, unlike micros in many other countries, did not identify themselves as disproportionately constrained by either the cost of or access to credit. The Salvadoran micros we sampled are predominantly oriented toward final consumers -- only 7% of their output went to larger domestic enterprises. This may indicate that microenterprises are not linked to larger firms through supply or subcontractual ties. If this is true, then policies that encourage the growth of larger enterprises may not directly benefit the growth of microenterprises (except insofar as they increase consumer demand for microenterprise goods and services).

Like their larger counterparts, *formal* microenterprises were moderately troubled by inflation and by problems of security. Formal microenterprises are moderately constrained by the state of roads and telephone service, and by insufficient demand. Regulations, however, impose either a minor or no constraint at all for formal microenterprises. *Informal* microenterprises are especially constrained by financing problems, which is their leading general concern. Unlike their formal counterparts, informal microenterprises find both collateral requirements and interest rates moderately constraining, and perceive their lack of adequate connections to banks and bankers a moderate constraint. Informal microenterprises are also particularly constrained by their problems in accessing space or land to run their businesses (a major constraint), by power supply problems (moderate), and by a general lack of demand (a moderate difficulty, but nonetheless ranked higher than by formal firms). However, informals are remarkably unconcerned with security and, as might be expected, find regulations no problem at all.

Exporters. Further analysis determined the differences in problems faced by major exporters (here defined by those enterprises that export 25% or more of their production), minor exporters (here defined as those that exported something less than 25% of production) and non-exporters (who exclusively supply the domestic market). In general, those firms that export 25% or more of their sales rank leading constraints lower than do other firms. Non-exporters are most constrained by inflation and price instability. Minor exporters feel most acutely affected by political and policy uncertainty, and by the level of the exchange rate. This may indicate that those firms just entering export activity are more sensitive to these factors, hence export growth is critically dependent on stable economic policies and a consistent policy regime. Minor exporters also identify themselves as more constrained by informal competition than do other firms, particularly in the areas of competitors avoiding taxes, trade regulations, and labor regulations, and in competitors undercutting their prices and offering goods of a lesser quality than they advertise. Major exporters also find informal competition constraining, and are somewhat more constrained than other firms by competitors selling below international prices. In regulation, there are few differences to report and all no category of regulation imposes more than a minor constraint, but minor exporters are a bit more constrained than other firms by required permits, customs procedures, and other import procedures.

In the area of infrastructure, minor exporters are also much more constrained by the state of roads than are major- and non-exporting firms. Major exporters, which tend to be larger firms, are more likely to have their own generator (58% do) and to use radios to augment the telephone system. Given these investments, it is not surprising that they are no more constrained by power concerns and less constrained by telecommunications than other firms. Beyond basic communication, however, fewer major exporters (16%) than other firms (21%) identified telecommunication services they would like but could not obtain. And there was some indication that international transport and telecommunications services are better than domestic transport: major exporters were less likely than other firms to complain that transport and telecom created problems in meeting commitments to customers. In addition, while firms report having to make 3.9 attempts to complete a local call, they average only 2.3 attempts per completed international call.

Responses to questions on technology, production and business services suggest the difficulties some firms may face in reaching international technical standards. Minor exporters found greater difficulties (although still moderate to minor) than major exporters or nonexporters in meeting orders in a timely way, in accessing information on new products, technology and equipment suppliers, in obtaining foreign technology, in finding qualified technicians, and in obtaining market information.

Industrial Subsectors. Finally, responses were disaggregated by industrial subsector to determine if, although, overall, firms found no constraint more than moderate, particular sectors did encounter major or severe constraints. This disaggregation made clear that a number of traditional sectors are relatively untroubled. For example, for the food, drink and tobacco, textile, and leather and footwear products sectors, the only moderate obstacle was inflation/price instability. For the clothing manufacture industry, only financial problems were considered moderate. By contrast, there were numerous moderate and even major constraints identified by the chemical industry, led by the fertilizer and pesticide subsector which found regulations, inflation and the functioning of the judicial system each to impose major obstacles. The chemicals sector generally led other sectors in concerns about inflation, policy uncertainty and security. The pesticide and fertilizer subsector and the machinery and equipment subsector each had greater difficulties in the business dealings with the government than did other sectors. Both found the slow process between tendering and contract award and the excessive bureaucracy and permits involved in supplying public agencies to be major obstacles, while the machinery subsector also found late payment to be a major problem. Informal competition imposed major constraints on four subsectors: shoes and leather, medicine and cosmetics, other chemicals, and machinery and equipment. Each had major difficulties with competitors avoiding taxes, and three of four encounter major problems with competitors evading trade laws and labor laws. Medicine and cosmetics companies had particular problems with competitors fraudulent or misleading claims for their products and with competitors selling below international prices (dumping). Machinery and equipment respondents sector was especially constrained with competitors selling below their own costs.

Although regulation was generally not constraining, fertilizer and pesticide companies felt that the permits and licenses required of them and tax regulations each imposed major constraints. Finally, infrastructure appear to constrain paper products manufacturers the most: they found energy supply, telecommunications and roads each to be major constraints. The subsectors manufacturing fertilizer and pesticide and medicine and cosmetics also found roads to impose a major constraint, while other chemical companies found telecom a major limitation. In finance, the fertilizer and pesticide and other chemicals subsectors were disproportionately constrained by interest rates. In technology and business service issues, machinery and equipment producers found it especially difficult to access foreign technology, fertilizer and pesticide producers found lack of domestic market information and major constraint, and machinery and equipment producers were similarly constrained by lack of export market information.

BIBLIOGRAPHY

Andic, S. (1992), "El Salvador: Tax System and Its Reform," Washington D.C.: Report prepared for the World Bank.

_____. (1993), "A Review of El Salvador's Tax System," Washington D.C.: Report prepared for the World Bank.

Azam, J.P., D. Bevan, P. Collier, S. Dercon, J. Gunning, and S. Pradhan (1994), "Some Economic Consequences of the Transition from Civil War to Peace," The World Bank - Policy Research Working Paper #1392 (December).

Bennett, Adam G. G. (1994), "Currency Boards: Issues and Experiences," IMF Paper on Policy Analysis and Assessment (September).

Calvo, G., L. Leiderman, and C. Reinhart (1993), "The Capital Inflows Problem: Concepts and Issues," IMF Paper on Policy Analysis and Assessment (July).

Calvo, G., and C. A. Végh (1992), "Currency Substitution in Developing Countries: An Introduction," IMF Working Paper (May).

Corbo, V. and L. Hernández (1994), "Macroeconomic Adjustment to Capital Inflows - Latin American Style versus East Asian Style," World Bank - Policy Research Working Paper #1377 (November).

Corden, W.M. (1984), "Booming Sector and Dutch Disease Economics: Survey and Consolidation," Oxford Economics Papers 36(3): 359-80.

Corden, W.M., and J.P. Neary (1992), "Booming Sector and De-Industrialization in a Small Open Economy," Economic Journal (92): 825-48.

Edwards, S. (1995), "Why are Savings Rates so Different Across Countries? An International Comparative Analysis," NBER Working Paper Series (5097).

_____. (1993), "Exchange Rates as Nominal Anchors," Weltwirtschaftliches Archiv (129): 1-33.

_____. (1989), Real Exchange Rates, Devaluation and Adjustment. Exchange Rate Policy in Developing Countries. Cambridge, Mass: MIT Press.

_____. (1986), "A Commodity Export Boom and the Real Exchange Rate: The Money-Inflation Link," in J. Neary and S. van Wijnbergen, eds. Natural Resources and the Macroeconomy. Cambridge, Mass: MIT Press.

_____. (1984), "Commodity Export Prices and the Real Exchange Rate in Developing Countries: Coffee in Colombia," in S. Edwards and L. Ahamed (eds.) Economic Adjustment and Exchange Rates in Developing Countries. Chicago: University of Chicago Press.

Frankel, J. A. (1994), "Sterilization of Money Inflows: Difficult (Calvo) or Easy (Resien)?" IMF Paper on Policy Analysis and Assessment (December).

FUSADES (1993), "Desafíos de la Reconversión Industrial," Boletín Económico y Social #96 (November).

_____. (1994), "La Emigración de Salvadoreños y su Impacto Económico y Social," Boletín Económico y Social # 98 (January).

_____. (1995), "La Empresa y el Reto de la Globalización," Boletín Económico y Social #110 (January).

Gregory, P. (1993), "The Labor Market of El Salvador," Report prepared for USAID (April).

Hanson, R. J. (1993),. "An Assessment of the Legal and Regulatory Framework for Enterprises in El Salvador." Report prepared for the IDB, Washington, D.C. (October).

Harberger, A. C. (1993), "Las Exportaciones y El Tipo de Cambio Real en El Salvador". Report prepared for FUSADES (October).

_____. (1995), "Reflections on the Economy of El Salvador," Report prepared for FUSADES (June).

IDB (1991), El Salvador: Private Investment Diagnostic Study (October).

Leamer, E.E., A. Guerra, M. Kaufman, and B. Segura (1995), "How does the North American Free Trade Agreement Affect Central America?" World Bank - Policy Research Working Paper #1464 (May).

Lopez, J.R. and M. A. Seligson (1991), "Small Business Development in El Salvador: The Impact of Remittances," in S. Diaz-Briquets and S. Weintraub, eds. Migration, Remittances, and Small Business Development: Mexico and Caribbean Basin Countires. Boulder, Co: Westview Press.

Montes, S. and J.J. Garcia Vasquez (1988), Salvadoran Migration to the United States: An Exploratory Study Washington D.C.: Georgetown University.

Nathan Associates, Inc. (1994), "El Salvador: Revision of Laws Governing International Trade and Investment," Report prepared for USAID (June).

Nehru, V. and A. Dhareshwar (1994), "New Estimates of Total Factor Productivity Growth for Developing and Industrial Countries," World Bank - Policy Research Working Paper #1313 (November).

Rajapatirana, S. (1993), Policy Recommendations for Export Promotion, paper presented at the Annual Meeting of the Chilean economic Society held on May 7-8, 1993.

Talley, S. (1994), "Deposit Protection and the Spread of Deposit Insurance - Some Guidelines for Developing Countries," World Bank FPD Note #12, (June).

van Wijnbergen, S. (1984), The "Dutch Disease:" A Disease after All?," <u>The Economic Journal</u> 94 (May):41-55.

Wang. Y. and J. Schilling (1995), "Managing Capital Flows in East Asia," <u>World Bank Discussion Paper</u>, Washington D.C.: The World Bank.

Webster, L. (1994), "Lending for Microenterprises - A Review of the World Bank's Portfolio," <u>World Bank FPD Note</u> #12. (June).

World Bank (1995), <u>Global Economic Prospects and the Developing Countries,</u> Washington, D.C.: World Bank.

_____. (1993), <u>The Asian Miracle - Economic Growth and Public Policy,</u> Washington, D.C.: World Bank.

_____. (1991a), <u>World Development Report</u> Washington, D.C.: World Bank.

_____. (1991b), <u>Developing the Private Sector, The World Bank's Experience and Approach</u> Washington D.C.: World Bank.

Younger, S. D. (1992). "Aid and the Dutch Disease: Macroeconomic Management When Everybody Loves You," <u>World Development</u> 20 (11): 1587-97.

Distributors of World Bank Publications

Prices and credit terms vary from country to country. Consult your local distributor before placing an order.

ALBANIA
Adrion Ltd.
Perlat Rexhepi Str.
Pall. 9, Shk. 1, Ap. 4
Tirana
Tel: (42) 274 19; 221 72
Fax: (42) 274 19

ARGENTINA
Oficina del Libro Internacional
Av. Cordoba 1877
1120 Buenos Aires
Tel: (1) 815-8156
Fax: (1) 815-8354

AUSTRALIA, FIJI, PAPUA NEW GUINEA, SOLOMON ISLANDS, VANUATU, AND WESTERN SAMOA
D.A. Information Services
648 Whitehorse Road
Mitcham 3132
Victoria
Tel: (61) 3 9210 7777
Fax: (61) 3 9210 7788
URL: http://www.dadirect.com.au

AUSTRIA
Gerold and Co.
Graben 31
A-1011 Wien
Tel: (1) 533-50-14-0
Fax: (1) 512-47-31-29

BANGLADESH
Micro Industries Development
Assistance Society (MIDAS)
House 5, Road 16
Dhanmondi R/Area
Dhaka 1209
Tel: (2) 326427
Fax: (2) 811188

BELGIUM
Jean De Lannoy
Av. du Roi 202
1060 Brussels
Tel: (2) 538-5169
Fax: (2) 538-0841

BRAZIL
Publicaões Tecnicas Internacionais
Lda.
Rua Peixoto Gomide, 209
01409 Sao Paulo, SP.
Tel: (11) 259-6644
Fax: (11) 258-6990

CANADA
Renouf Publishing Co. Ltd.
1294 Algoma Road
Ottawa, Ontario K1B 3W8
Tel: 613-741-4333
Fax: 613-741-5439

CHINA
China Financial & Economic
Publishing House
8, Da Fo Si Dong Jie
Beijing
Tel: (1) 333-8257
Fax: (1) 401-7365

COLOMBIA
Infoenlace Ltda.
Apartado Aereo 34270
Bogotá D.E.
Tel: (1) 285-2798
Fax: (1) 285-2798

COTE D'IVOIRE
Centre d'Edition et de Diffusion
Africaines (CEDA)
04 B.P. 541
Abidjan 04 Plateau
Tel: 225-24-6510
Fax: 225-25-0567

CYPRUS
Center of Applied Research
Cyprus College
6, Diogenes Street, Engomi
P.O. Box 2006
Nicosia
Tel: 244-1730
Fax: 246-2051

CZECH REPUBLIC
National Information Center
prodejna, Konviktska 5
CS – 113 57 Prague 1
Tel: (2) 2422-9433
Fax: (2) 2422-1484
URL: http://www.nis.cz/

DENMARK
SamfundsLitteratur
Rosenoerns Allé 11
DK-1970 Frederiksberg C
Tel: (31)-351942
Fax: (31)-357822

EGYPT, ARAB REPUBLIC OF
Al Ahram
Al Galaa Street
Cairo
Tel: (2) 578-6083
Fax: (2) 578-6833

The Middle East Observer
41, Sherif Street
Cairo
Tel: (2) 393-9732
Fax: (2) 393-9732

FINLAND
Akateeminen Kirjakauppa
P.O. Box 23
FIN-00371 Helsinki
Tel: (0) 12141
Fax: (0) 121-4441
URL: http://booknet.cultnet.fi/aka/

FRANCE
World Bank Publications
66, avenue d'Iéna
75116 Paris
Tel: (1) 40-69-30-56/57
Fax: (1) 40-69-30-68

GERMANY
UNO-Verlag
Poppelsdorfer Allee 55
53115 Bonn
Tel: (228) 212940
Fax: (228) 217492

GREECE
Papasotiriou S.A.
35, Stournara Str.
106 82 Athens
Tel: (1) 364-1826
Fax: (1) 364-8254

HONG KONG, MACAO
Asia 2000 Ltd.
Sales & Circulation Department
Seabird House, unit 1101-02
22-28 Wyndham Street, Central
Hong Kong
Tel: 852 2530-1409
Fax: 852 2526-1107
URL: http://www.sales@asia2000.com.hk

HUNGARY
Foundation for Market
Economy
Dombovari Ut 17-19
H-1117 Budapest
Tel: 36 1 204 2951 or
36 1 204 2948
Fax: 36 1 204 2953

INDIA
Allied Publishers Ltd.
751 Mount Road
Madras - 600 002
Tel: (44) 852-3938
Fax: (44) 852-0649

INDONESIA
Pt. Indira Limited
Jalan Borobudur 20
P.O. Box 181
Jakarta 10320
Tel: (21) 390-4290
Fax: (21) 421-4289

IRAN
Kowkab Publishers
P.O. Box 19575-511
Tehran
Tel: (21) 258-3723
Fax: 98 (21) 258-3723

Ketab Sara Co. Publishers
Khaled Eslamboli Ave.,
6th Street
Kusheh Delafrooz No. 8
Tehran
Tel: 8717819 or 8716104
Fax: 8862479

IRELAND
Government Supplies Agency
Oifig an tSoláthair
4-5 Harcourt Road
Dublin 2
Tel: (1) 461-3111
Fax: (1) 475-2670

ISRAEL
Yozmot Literature Ltd.
P.O. Box 56055
Tel Aviv 61560
Tel: (3) 5285-397
Fax: (3) 5285-397

R.O.Y. International
PO Box 13056
Tel Aviv 61130
Tel: (3) 5461423
Fax: (3) 5461442

Palestinian Authority/Middle East
Index Information Services
P.O.B. 19502 Jerusalem
Tel: (2) 271219

ITALY
Licosa Commissionaria Sansoni SPA
Via Duca Di Calabria, 1/1
Casella Postale 552
50125 Firenze
Tel: (55) 645-415
Fax: (55) 641-257

JAMAICA
Ian Randle Publishers Ltd.
206 Old Hope Road
Kingston 6
Tel: 809-927-2085
Fax: 809-977-0243

JAPAN
Eastern Book Service
Hongo 3-Chome,
Bunkyo-ku 113
Tokyo
Tel: (03) 3818-0861
Fax: (03) 3818-0864
URL: http://www.bekkoame.or.jp/~svt-ebs

KENYA
Africa Book Service (E.A.) Ltd.
Quaran House, Mfangano Street
P.O. Box 45245
Nairobi
Tel: (2) 23641
Fax: (2) 330272

KOREA, REPUBLIC OF
Daejon Trading Co. Ltd.
P.O. Box 34
Yeoeida
Seoul
Tel: (2) 785-1631/4
Fax: (2) 784-0315

MALAYSIA
University of Malaya Cooperative
Bookshop, Limited
P.O. Box 1127
Jalan Pantai Baru
59700 Kuala Lumpur
Tel: (3) 756-5000
Fax: (3) 755-4424

MEXICO
INFOTEC
Apartado Postal 22-860
14060 Tlalpan,
Mexico D.F.
Tel: (5) 606-0011
Fax: (5) 606-0386

NETHERLANDS
De Lindeboom/InOr-Publikaties
P.O. Box 202
7480 AE Haaksbergen
Tel: (53) 574-0004
Fax: (53) 572-9296

NEW ZEALAND
EBSCO NZ Ltd.
Private Mail Bag 99914
New Market
Auckland
Tel: (9) 524-8119
Fax: (9) 524-8067

NIGERIA
University Press Limited
Three Crowns Building Jericho
Private Mail Bag 5095
Ibadan
Tel: (22) 41-1356
Fax: (22) 41-2056

NORWAY
Narvesen Information Center
Book Department
P.O. Box 6125 Etterstad
N-0602 Oslo 6
Tel: (22) 57-3300
Fax: (22) 68-1901

PAKISTAN
Mirza Book Agency
65, Shahrah-e-Quaid-e-Azam
P.O. Box No. 729
Lahore 54000
Tel: (42) 7353601
Fax: (42) 7585283

Oxford University Press
5 Bangalore Town
Sharae Faisal
PO Box 13033
Karachi-75350
Tel: (21) 446307
Fax: (21) 454-7640

PERU
Editorial Desarrollo SA
Apartado 3824
Lima 1
Tel: (14) 285380
Fax: (14) 286628

PHILIPPINES
International Booksource Center Inc.
Suite 720, Cityland 10
Condominium Tower 2
H.V. dela Costa, corner
Valero St.
Makati, Metro Manila
Tel: (2) 817-9676
Fax: (2) 817-1741

POLAND
International Publishing Service
Ul. Piekna 31/37
00-577 Warzawa
Tel: (2) 628-6089
Fax: (2) 621-7255

PORTUGAL
Livraria Portugal
Rua Do Carmo 70-74
1200 Lisbon
Tel: (1) 347-4982
Fax: (1) 347-0264

ROMANIA
Compani De Librari Bucuresti S.A.
Str. Lipscani no. 26, sector 3
Bucharest
Tel: (1) 613 9645
Fax: (1) 312 4000

RUSSIAN FEDERATION
Isdatelstvo <Ves Mir>
9a, Kolpachniy Pereulok
Moscow 101831
Tel: (95) 917 87 49
Fax: (95) 917 92 59

SAUDI ARABIA, QATAR
Jarir Book Store
P.O. Box 3196
Riyadh 11471
Tel: (1) 477-3140
Fax: (1) 477-2940

SINGAPORE, TAIWAN, MYANMAR, BRUNEI
Asahgate Publishing Asia
Pacific Pte. Ltd.
41 Kallang Pudding Road #04-03
Golden Wheel Building
Singapore 349316
Tel: (65) 741-5166
Fax: (65) 742-9356
e-mail: ashgate@asianconnect.com

SLOVAK REPUBLIC
Slovart G.T.G. Ltd.
Krupinska 4
PO Box 152
852 99 Bratislava 5
Tel: (7) 839472
Fax: (7) 839485

SOUTH AFRICA, BOTSWANA
For single titles:
Oxford University Press
Southern Africa
P.O. Box 1141
Cape Town 8000
Tel: (21) 45-7266
Fax: (21) 45-7265

For subscription orders:
International Subscription Service
P.O. Box 41095
Craighall
Johannesburg 2024
Tel: (11) 880-1448
Fax: (11) 880-6248

SPAIN
Mundi-Prensa Libros, S.A.
Castello 37
28001 Madrid
Tel: (1) 431-3399
Fax: (1) 575-3998
http://www.tsai.es/mprensa

Mundi-Prensa Barcelona
Consell de Cent, 391
08009 Barcelona
Tel: (3) 488-3009
Fax: (3) 487-7659

SRI LANKA, THE MALDIVES
Lake House Bookshop
P.O. Box 244
100, Sir Chittampalam A.
Gardiner Mawatha
Colombo 2
Tel: (1) 32105
Fax: (1) 432104

SWEDEN
Fritzes Customer Service
Regeringsgatan 12
S-106 47 Stockholm
Tel: (8) 690 90 90
Fax: (8) 21 47 77

Wennergren-Williams AB
P.O. Box 1305
S-171 25 Solna
Tel: (8) 705-97-50
Fax: (8) 27-00-71

SWITZERLAND
Librairie Payot
Service Institutionnel
Côtes-de-Montbenon 30
1002 Lausanne
Tel: (021)-341-3229
Fax: (021)-341-3235

Van Diermen Editions Techniq
Ch. de Lacuez 41
CH1807 Blonay
Tel: (021) 943 2673
Fax: (021) 943 3605

TANZANIA
Oxford University Press
Maktaba Street
PO Box 5299
Dar es Salaam
Tel: (51) 29209
Fax: (51) 46822

THAILAND
Central Books Distribution
306 Silom Road
Bangkok
Tel: (2) 235-5400
Fax: (2) 237-8321

TRINIDAD & TOBAGO, JAM.
Systematics Studies Unit
#9 Watts Street
Curepe
Trinidad, West Indies
Tel: 809-662-5654
Fax: 809-662-5654

UGANDA
Gustro Ltd.
Madhvani Building
PO Box 9997
Plot 16/4 Jinja Rd.
Kampala
Tel/Fax: (41) 254763

UNITED KINGDOM
Microinfo Ltd.
P.O. Box 3
Alton, Hampshire GU34 2PG
England
Tel: (1420) 86848
Fax: (1420) 89889

ZAMBIA
University Bookshop
Great East Road Campus
P.O. Box 32379
Lusaka
Tel: (1) 213221 Ext. 482

ZIMBABWE
Longman Zimbabwe (Pte.)Ltd.
Tourle Road, Ardbennie
P.O. Box ST125
Southerton
Harare
Tel: (4) 6216617
Fax: (4) 621670